She Got Away With It

Aimee Bell

Published by Trellis Publishing, 2021.

While every precaution has been taken in the preparation of this book, the publisher assumes no responsibility for errors or omissions, or for damages resulting from the use of the information contained herein.

SHE GOT AWAY WITH IT

First edition. July 12, 2021.

Copyright © 2021 Aimee Bell.

ISBN: 979-8224319008

Written by Aimee Bell.

SHE GOT AWAY WITH IT

EMMY BELL

Debra Lynn Baker seemed to have scored the perfect job. She had no skills to speak of but called herself a "fast learner" when she interviewed for the position of bookkeeper for millionaire Jerry Sternadel. A close friend of his wife, the two allegedly began embezzling money from Sternadel's business, causing numerous checks to bounce. Sternadel caught wind of the embezzlement and threatened legal action. He died under mysterious circumstances weeks later with the money still outstanding. Who stole the money and why have they not been prosecuted?

Debra's background

Debra Lynn Baker's early life seemed idyllic. She grew up in the peacefulness of Wichita, Texas, marrying her childhood sweetheart Tony in 1975. The couple would have a son, Charles, who would go on to become a star football player in high school.

In 1982, Debra Lynn's best friend, Lou Ann, would marry Jerry Sternadel. Jerry was a divorced multi-millionaire. A business mogul, he owned real estate, a plumbing business as well as having his own horse racing stable. Jerry was a sex addict, however, with countless mistresses which included his own step-daughter.

WORKING AT THE RANCH

As his business grew, Jerry needed some help with his accounting. He needed a bookkeeper and began looking to hire someone. Lou Ann thought that this was the perfect chance to help her best friend, Debra. She sold her husband on Debra's employability even though she did not have any accounting experience. Jerry reluctantly agreed and hired her formally as his bookkeeper and business manager. Debra was ecstatic. Things were going well in her marriage, she now had a well-paying job and could see her best friend on a daily basis.

Jerry also gave Debra and her family a house down the road from his ranch. He wanted her to be as available as she could for all the work he needed to be done. Even with this, Debra was rarely home as she was almost full-time at Jerry and Lou Ann's ranch doing the books...

Debra and Lou Ann spent almost every waking moment together. They ate each and every lunch together and even worked at the same office in the ranch. They also frequently traveled together. "We were together 5 days a week," Debra said. Jerry began to suspect that the duo were more than just "friends".

ANGRY JERRY

This arrangement would last eight years. Jerry's businesses were thriving but he became increasingly difficult to deal with. His first wife, Jeanie Walker, would confirm that Jerry's "abrasive manner grew with his wealth."

"Jerry was extremely hard on his family," Debra said. "Extremely hard on his kids."

Jerry began treating his workers, and even his family, horribly for no apparent reason.

"Jerry said if you have money you can do anything you want to do," Walker said. "And you can tell anybody else to do whatever you want them to do."

Both Lou Ann and Debra Lynn felt increasingly annoyed by Jerry's presence in their lives and discussed that frequently. It was a hate triangle. Jerry hated Lou Ann and wished to divorce her. Debra hated Jerry, her boss, so did Lou Ann. But they didn't hate the extravagant lifestyle that he afforded them.

One day, the volatile Jerry exploded into a fit of rage that was out of the ordinary for even him. A check had bounced from his account, the first time that ever happened in his business life. Growing suspicious of the cause, he hired an auditor to go through all of his accounts and bills.

The auditor confirmed his suspicions.

He discovered that $35,000 was missing from one account and transferred to Debra Lynn's account.

"He told me there was over $100,000 that he found real quick," Jeanie Walker said. "He said he wanted the money back or I'm going to have her arrested for embezzlement."

Jerry thought both Debra Lynn and Lou Ann were complicit. He confronted them both about the missing money and gave them an ultimatum. Either give the money back by the upcoming Memorial Day or he would inform the police of their embezzlement.

He then threatened Lou Ann with divorce.

SICK JERRY

The following day Jerry had lunch with Lou Ann and Debra at his ranch, as the trio normally did. Within an hour, Jerry began experiencing severe stomach pain. The food began coming out of both ends, as he began to vomit and shit uncontrollably. Jerry would be hospitalized and began suffering from paranoid delusions, screaming that the doctors were trying to kill him.

Curiously, Tom Bradley, a nineteen-year-old house guest had drunk some Cranberry juice from Jerry's refrigerator and within minutes suffered from the same symptoms Jerry had.

Meanwhile, the emergency room doctors scratched their heads about Jerry's symptoms. They could not understand how an active and energetic man could be dying right in front of their eyes.

Jerry would be released from the hospital but in the ensuing weeks, he would be brought back three more times. The women had not given him his money back and now Jerry was convinced they were trying to poison him. Lou Ann, however, gave all of the doctors a wink and a nod.

"He's hallucinating," she whispered. "He's crazy."

"Please help me!" Jerry cried out as the emergency room technicians strapped his wrists to the gurney. "Cut me loose! I don't want to die! Those two women are killing me!"

Jerry would be released from the hospital but died in his home on June 12th, 1990.

WHAT HAPPENED?

An autopsy showed that Jerry did not die from a mysterious virus but he had consumed a more-than-deadly dose of arsenic given to him over an extended period. At a determinate dose, arsenic is lethal: When it enters in your system, there's no way back, it's time for your last prayers.

The forensic doctors determined that Jerry had sipped small doses of arsenic over a period of time until the levels continued to rise in his bloodstream. He was poisoned to death.

Lou Ann didn't cry when she was informed of Jerry's death.

She did not even try to pretend she was sorrowful. Their mutual hate was well-known, but she acted indifferently. Yet, Debra Lynn's reaction was curious to say the least: She got eerily anxious and disturbed. When the doctors let her know about Jerry's death, she ran past everyone through the hospital aisles to the elevator. What made her so nervous?

At Jerry's funeral, Lou Ann was as upbeat and lively as you can get, bouncing off the walls as if she had gulped down a six-pack of Red Bull. She chatted with her friends and laughed uproariously at the slightest attempt at humor.

She had good reason to be happy. She was now the primary beneficiary of the ranch, Jerry's businesses, and a $350,000 life insurance policy.

Her extravagant lifestyle was assured even with Jerry gone.

ENTER TOM BRADLEY

Tom Bradley, the young house guest, revealed to police how he had gotten sick after drinking Jerry's cranberry juice. He was invited to do a blood test and the results came back positive from arsenic levels. Then, after this, the police started to investigate the case deeper to discover where the poison came from. It was traced to a bottle of cranberry juice -Jerry's favorite, the one Tom Bradley also drank and got sick- that was in a trash bag on the Sternadel estate.

They were able to trace it since they found the trash bag buried in the yard with the bottle inside. The bottle had soap bubbles which indicated someone tried to wash it before throwing it away. Yet, the bottle was sloppily cleaned, so the police officers could test the bottle and found the arsenic traces. Bingo.

At the moment it was more than evident that Jerry was poisoned to death. But who was it? Lou Ann? Debra?

In 1991, Debra, Lou Ann, and Tony moved to San Marcos and began a trucking business with Jerry's life insurance money. Interestingly, only two years after Jerry's death, someone stopped paying rent on a storage unit in Wichita Falls, Debra Lynn Baker, and Tony Baker's hometown. When the owner went into the unit, he found tons documents and bills belonging to Jerry Sternadel. He called the police as the case of Jerry Sternadel was well known among locals.

The cops went to the unit and found a huge bottle of arsenic poison for rats. The unit was registered to a Kathy Simmons but had the direction of Debra Lynn Baker in Holiday, Texas. That was all the evidence the police required to arrest Debra, placing her in custody on May 14, 1993.

Even though Lou Ann was a suspect of being an accomplice of Jerry's murder, Debra declined to incriminate her best friend. The police tried to pressure her into giving Lou Ann up, bringing up the fact that she would be brought to trial for murder in first degree. The sentence could result in life in prison but she refused to blow the whistle on her best friend.

Debra Lynn Baker's trial

On January 18th, 1994 Debra went on trial for first-degree murder. She stole the money, so she had the motive. She had the arsenic, so she had the means and she virtually lived in Jerry's ranch so she certainly had the opportunity.

The prosecutors gave a depiction of a hate triangle rather than a love triangle despite the claims that Lou Ann and Debra were more than friends. Jerry hated his wife, Debra hated her boss and Lou Ann hated her husband. Each of the women feared the possibility of losing the extravagant lifestyle. Prosecutors claimed that Debra decided to poison Jerry before he was able to divorce Lou Ann and before he would file charges about the $35,000.

The prosecuting attorney stated Debra had the arsenic used to kill Jerry in the storage shed registered with her address; she took the $30,000.00 from Jerry's bank account, and lastly, she was frequently in Jerry's home and was his wife's best friend. Moreover, the prosecutor proposed that poison is typically a female's way of committing a homicide as it is a detached technique that permits the assassin to say to herself, "I haven't killed him; the poison has."

The defense claimed there was no evidence the storage unit was of Debra's property and her fingerprints were not found on the arsenic bottle. Her attorney then detailed Jerry's explosive and abrasive character, bringing numerous witnesses to testify against him to show he had won countless enemies throughout his life and a lot of other people had reasons to poison him aside from Debra.

The Aftermath

Debra was found guilty of murder in first degree, based mainly on the bottle of arsenic found in the storage unit registered at her address. Debra Lynn Baker poisoned Jerry by putting arsenic in his cranberry juice, as an expert who testified in the trial proofed. Jerry was given three different doses of the poison before finally dying on June 1990 at the United Regional Hospital. Debra, as Jerry suspected, was stealing money from Sternadel's accounts with forged checks, and Tim Cole –the Clay County District Attorney at that time- used that as her main motive in the prosecution.

"It was old-fashioned greed," Jeannie Walker said. "Money became more important than anything."

When the verdict of guilty was announced, Debra's husband became enraged and lunged at the jurors. The deputy sheriff had to hold him down. But he didn't hold him down for long. The following day the jury suggested Debra be given ten years of probation and a ten thousand dollar fine.

Prosecutor Tim Cole was stunned at the leniency of the verdict.

"It was a case that was not the strongest on the evidence," Cole said. "It was a circumstantial case (...) so we were pleased that we got the conviction, but not so happy with the punishment the jury assessed."

Debra Lynn Baker and her husband had moved to Hays County before the trial. She found a job as a bookkeeper with another rancher and in 1993 she was charged with forging two checks of $3,200 by a Hays County Grand Jury. But the case didn't go to court until after she had already been given probation for the first-degree murder charge so the judge said he could not give her another probation for forgery as she was already serving her sentence for the murder.

So, she served 10 years of probation for stealing almost $ 40,000 and killing a man. Everything is bigger in Texas, even surprises.

WHAT ABOUT LOU ANN?

As it was said before, Lou Ann's lack of emotional response to her husband's death has always been suspicious.

She didn't appear in court for a single day of Debra's trial.

The prosecutor's theory was that both Lou Ann and Debra conspired to murder Jerry for his inheritance and life insurance money. Debra was found guilty, but why wasn't Lou Ann investigated?

"When we got the outcome we did in the Baker case," prosecutor Tim Cole said. "We didn't go forward with any case on the wife because it would have been probably the same or maybe a worse result".

"I talked to jurors about why they would give her probation," Jeanie Walker's first wife said. "They said they felt she was the scapegoat, that the widow was the one who had committed the crime."

Another problem was that Jerry was never able to investigate if the money robbery was conducted by Debra Lynn Baker herself, the prosecutor could not use that as a motive. Rather, he used a much more wobbly motive: that Debra killed Jerry Sternadel so he could not divorce Lou Ann and she wouldn't lose her rights to Jerry's inheritance. Yet, the jury could not deny the fact that arsenic was found in a storage unit owned by Debra Lynn Baker using a false ID. They believe she was a stooge rather than the leader of the operation.

KARMA?

So Debra Lynn Baker walked free with a little probation sentence. Lou Ann gets nothing more than suspicion and all of the inheritance.

But stupid is as stupid does. Debra Lynn Baker could not stay out of trouble for long.

By 1999, Baker forged another check, violating her probation. She received another lenient sentence but by 2002, the prosecutor revoked her probation. By December 2003, Debra Lynn Baker was finally sent to prison.

Nine years after the trial Debra finally goes to prison for...Ten years.

But she was up for parole the following year and Jerry's family seized their right to communicate with the parole board. They energetically opposed to her release. Jeannie Walker became the leader of the movement to serve justice for her ex-husband, wanting their two children to see justice served. She started an effective letter-writing crusade and the board listened...for a little while.

FREE AGAIN

Debra would be released from the Carole Young unit in Galveston County of Texas Department of Criminal Justice on June 20th, 2013. She was fifty-six years old at the time. Becky Sternadel, Jerry's oldest daughter, said she was going to continue seeking justice for her father. "No, I don't think justice has been served (...) Texas prides itself on being hard on crime yet a convicted murderer gets ten years probation. The criminal justice system in Texas has failed the Sternadel family since 1990"

"I don't honestly know what my reaction would be if I ever was to actually see her face to face but I did write her a letter to her in prison,"

Becky said. "I don't know if she got the letter or not. I told her I would never stop ever until she serves the rest of her life in prison."

Family members, including Becky and Jeannie, believe Lou Ann Sternadel had a major role in Jerry's murder but, as we already know, she was never charged. By the time Becky hoped that Debra Baker's released would bring additional evidence to surface linking Lou Ann to Sternadel's murder. To this day nothing new has happened.

"I would like to see the death penalty be given to Lou Ann," Becky said to the press the day Debra was released. "I want her to be tried and convicted before a court and I want her to be sentenced to death, just like she did my dad. I don't know if there will ever be closure, I mean, you can't bring my father back but I think God has the ultimate power on that one."

The mystery remains

As for today, the Sternadel family campaign, led by Jerry's ex-wife, Jeannie Walker continues to ask the Governor of Texas to contemplate every means possible to reopen the case and serve justice for the murder of Jerry. Lou Ann pretended to be a caring wife, as she and her best friend, Debra Baker, continued serving her husband food and drink mixed with arsenic venom.

It remains to be seen if, one day, justice will be served for Jerry Sternadel memory and family.

The whereabouts of Debra and Lou Ann are now unknown.

PIN UP QUEEN KILLER :

THE TRUE STORY OF SAMANTHA SCOTT

DALE CROWELL

Andrea Claire aka Samantha Scott had was born in 1941 and grew up in New Jersey.

At the age of 15, Andrea claimed that her mother forced her to marry the man who got her pregnant. In Andrea's words, she was rape but according to her mother, the 22-year old man got Andrea drunk and "took advantage." The man was a friend of her sister and reportedly was either set up on a date with her or picked her up from basketball practice.

Known to her friends as "Drea," Andrea would divorce the man after over two volatile years of abuse but the union still produced two children. Armed with only a 9th grade education, Andrea had no skill set and bounced from job to job. She began working as secretary, waitress, escrow worker, model and touring exotic dancer.

CAROUSEL OF MEN

She married again in a union that lasted three days as her new husband didn't want her to bring her children into the marriage (she met him while setting a trap to find out who was stealing her morning newspaper.) Her third marriage was to a Jordanian national who needed a wife in order to stay in the U.S.

"I married for a third time to a young Jordanian student," she said. "He had cousins in countries that he was afraid he'd be forced to fight against. This touched my heart and I figured 'What's the big deal?'"

They divorced after a few years when the student decided to marry his own childhood sweetheart.

She married a fourth time to a "con man" named Dereck who introduced her to his gay lover.

At some point, Andrea did give birth to a third child but put the baby up for adoption in 1961.

ACTING CAREER

In her mid-20s, Andrea got a few acting gigs, landing parts in M*A*S*H, Bewitched and the Russ Meyer T&A classic Beyond the Valley of the Dolls. She would be credited under the name of Samantha

Scott but would also use pseudonyms of Donna Duzzit, Sarah Stunning, and Prudence Smythe.

"She had been a bit player in a lot of TV shows and movies," Riverside County prosecutor James Hawkins said. "She had some beautiful photographs of herself. Facial, bathing suit, different costumes. She was in plays, movies."

Andrea got roles in some late 1960s "nudie cuties" like Horny Hobo, Wild Gypsies, Nude Django and Bad Girls for the Boys. She did manage two get a two episode run as "Betty" in the show Bewitched which would be the high water mark for her in Hollywood.

"She really couldn't make it as an actress," crime author Diane Fanning said. "So she ended up working as a call girl to make money."

Andrea had been thrown off a horse while filming a b-movie. She injured her back and claimed that this forced her into prostitution.

HIGH-PRICED CALL GIRL & DRUGS

"I was finally dating!" she said recalling her decision to become a call-girl. "I had read all Harold Robbins' books to learn about men and a lot of my dreams did come true through with these 'pay dates.'"

According to her probation report, Andrea began using marijuana in her late twenties and used until 1980. She also indulged in barbiturates and morphine based pain medication after she injured her back in the fall of the horse. During her time as a call-girl, she would use cocaine.

MORE MEN

In March of 1980, she married another man after a whirlwind ten-day courtship. The marriage did not last two weeks as her husband went into a jealous rage. Andrea was able to fend him off with a butcher knife, chasing him out of their Los Angeles apartment.

"Andrea was an exceptionally beautiful woman," forensic psychologist Oscar Newsome said. "I mean absolutely beautiful. She knew how to use her body and looks and words to seduce men and get them to do things for her. She was in several relationships and marriages, all short and quick."

DESPERATION TIME

Now in her late 30s, Andrea knew her days as a high-priced call girl would be numbered. She had to meet a "sugar daddy" and fast.

Enter lumber magnate Robert Sand, who at 69 years old was 30 years Andrea's senior.

"Robert Sand had been a lumberman in the northeast," Hawkins said. "He made a fortune there. Retired to Los Angeles. He also had a long standing history with prostitutes."

Sand had been confined to a wheelchair for years. He suffered from multiple sclerosis and was confined to a wheelchair.

Sand had married his first wife Frances in 1939 but they would divorce in 1947. Five years later, they would remarry. She first found out about her husband's proclivities for prostitutes in 1973 which effectively ended their sexual relationship but not the marriage.

"His wife was divorcing him because he had an $800 a week prostitute habit," Fanning said. "And she was just not comfortable with that and she leaves him. So that's how Andrea comes in Bob Sands life."

By December of 1980, Sand had finalized his divorce with Frances. Then he began living with Andrea.

The rich businessman found the sexy former actress and model irresistible. He booked her for repeated engagements as Andrea gave him sex and massages.

"It got to the point where it got so expensive that his accountant recommended that he stopped spending money on her each month and marry her," Hawkins said. "To save money."

"There was the sizable age difference, of course," forensic psychologist Oscar Newsome said. "And the two were introduced by Andrea's 'madam'. So obviously we're not talking the ideal marriage here. It is an arrangement at best."

The madam informed Andrea that Sand sometimes "played rough" but treated the women he sent to her well "in general."

Andrea's fourth divorce became final in December of 1980 and she then moved into Sand's apartment in Westwood where he asked for her hand in marriage. Andrea said "yes" and they moved to a condo at The Springs in Rancho Mirage.

"They lived in a big, gorgeous home," Fanning said. "In a very wealthy area in Rancho Mirage."

"Rancho Mirage is where a lot of political figures, CEOs, and actress and actors retire," Hawkins said. "Its known as the playground of the presidents."

RESPECTABILITY

Sand provided Andrea what she always wanted, respectability and security. They had famous people in their neighborhood like Tammy Faye Baker. So in the beginning, Andrea enjoyed herself.

She wheeled Robert around in his wheelchair as he watched her play golf and tennis. He took her shopping and she would continue to give him therapeutic massages.

"She did have a power over men," Hawkins said. "She had a way about her. She was very sensual. And she would, for lack of a better term, suck you in."

"Andrea Claire was pushing 40 years old," Newsome said. "She had to have seen the writing on the wall when it came to her stripping and call girl days. She wanted the easy life. The rich life. So when she came across Robert Sand she put her best foot forward. Here was a guy, stuck in a wheelchair and had literally money to burn. Most importantly, she knew that he had multiple sclerosis which would only get worse as time went on. She saw him as an opportunity. Marry the old man, wait until he becomes invalid or dies off then enjoy the benefits of his wealth."

CONTROL FREAK

Robert limited Andrea's social life, however. He was a sexual voyeur and made Andrea pose nude for photograph sessions and walk around their condo naked.

"Robert was an old man confined in a wheelchair," Newsome said. "So like most men in that position, he did not want any kind of competition for Andrea. So he kept her confined to the house. They wouldn't go out to eat. He wouldn't let her out, period. She rebelled, of course, but he really want her to be his on-call sex toy."

According to Andrea, Robert liked to spank her with a paddle and masturbated while he watched her have sex with other men. Andrea claimed that Robert became more and more demanding with his requests and fantasies. Every day the envelope was pushed further and further.

"I think her life would drastically change due to a marital contract that we found," Hawkins said. "She agreed to perform sexual services for him. There was a whole list of them. Some of them somewhat perverted. And he would follow her around and photograph her doing everything."

Robert's demands would be increasingly kinky as the months wore on.

"According to Andrea," Fanning said. "Bob got more and more sexually demanding. And the sex that he wanted was more and more sadistic."

MUTUAL ABUSE?

Robert would have complaints of his own, however. He informed his attorney friend that Andrea would routinely berate and insult him as well as leave him alone for long periods as she went off to "play tennis" and that she had a "terrible temper."

"Sand would complain that Andrea would be abusive," Newsome said. "It is unclear whether or not she would initiate the fights with him or she was responding to his own increasing demands. What is clear is that he got more than he bargained for when he married her as he didn't expect her to fight back or display such a temper."

Robert Sand, however, was not going to throw away a Rolls Royce just because it had a few dents in it.

"But he was also compelled to stay with her because she had the most incredible body he'd ever seen," Hawkins said. "And the sex was wonderful."

POISON THE OLD MAN?

With the arrangement becoming more and more intolerable, Andrea contacted a friend and asked him about the effects of Seconal. She said she had already tried to poison Robert and that it didn't work. She also told her tennis partner that her husband would soon die from multiple sclerosis. Her friend said that multiple sclerosis would not kill her husband, Andrea said, "No. He knows he's going to die very soon."

"Andrea had been a sexual plaything all of her life since the age of 15," Newsome said. "She saw Sand as her only way out and yet this was not going to be as easy as she thought. She began to feel resentful at first then it turned into outright hatred. The sexual games that he made her play, paddle boarding, sadomasochism. For even the most hardened prostitute, it all became too much for her."

"That may have been the straw that broke the camel's back," Hawkins said.

Andrea had enough. She wanted a marriage of convenience from a rapidly dying old man. Instead, she got nightly sexual humiliations from wheelchair bound pervert who didn't want a wife. He wanted a sex slave.

"She thought it would be a life of luxury," Hawkins said. "Instead it was a life of somewhat sexual slavery and she just couldn't stand it anymore. Even though Mr. Sand was in a wheelchair I think he was a very demanding person and he exorcised control over her primarily financially."

THE ATTACK

One night in May of 1981 it all came to a head.

Bob Sand laid on the bed, screaming at Andrea to come into the room and perform her sexual duties.

Andrea, however, had something else in mind.

"That's when she attacked him with the knife," Fanning said.

"It was an out of control frenzy," Hawkins said. "Just stabbing over and over and over again. He was stabbed over 27 times and importantly he was stabbed in the heart and severed the aorta."

"The attack was 'overkill' as one psychiatrist at the time described it," Newsome said. "She stabbed the man over twenty-seven times so this was a hate-filled, raging attack of someone who had a high amount of pent-up anger. All the rage and frustration Andrea felt at the humiliation she suffered, hell, maybe all of the rage she suffered for her whole life bubbled to the surface the moment she started stabbing Robert. And she didn't stop there. She picked up a wooden board that she used for exercise and slammed it down on his head so hard that it caused a fracture."

On May 14th, 1981 at 4 o'clock in the morning, security guards at The Springs investigated an alarm coming from the Sands' address. They found the front door open and were soon greeted by an upset Andrea in a black robe. She told the guards that there was a male intruder in the home and he had run out of the sliding glass door in the living room.

She led the guards into the bedroom where they saw the bloodied, nude body of Robert Sand.

Forty-five minutes later, Sheriff's Detective Fred Lastar arrived and the scene was secured. Andrea repeated the story of the intruder and she was allowed to go visit a neighbor.

Investigators would later establish that Sand had been stabbed 27 times and had been hit over the head several times with a 1' x 4' exercise board. There was in fact a trail of blood from the bedroom to the living room's sliding glass door but they found only a single bloodstain on the patio.

There were no footprints on the grass where Andrea said the intruder escaped.

Lastar also found it odd that in the master bathroom above the toilet there was a wet-t-shirt poster of Andrea with her nipples visible under the thin material.

Andrea would tell the Sheriff that she had taken some sleeping pills and had gone to bed early the previous night. She had heard her husband screaming for help and when she investigated she saw one or two men running out of the house.

"She said she heard her husband yelling out," Hawkins said. "She went down the hallway to his bedroom, she saw some stranger in the dark who bumped into her, pushed her out of the way and ran out of the condominium. She went in there to find Robert on the ground."

She looked and saw that Robert was dead. Oddly, she went and washed her clothes when they had gotten bloodied after she tried to help her husband. Even more strangely, Andrea then went back to sleep for two hours before calling security.

"The problem with Andrea's plan was that not only was she a bad actress," Newsome said. "She was a lousy screenwriter. She came up with this half-cocked story of intruders breaking in and stabbing her husband. Sand is a well-to-do retiree. The intruder takes nothing and leaves the buxom actress all alone to sort things through. Right away, the Sheriffs doubted her story. She implored for them to go out looking for the intruder but they found no signs of forced entry. Nothing that would indicate that a stranger had entered their home for the sole purpose of killing a rich old man in a wheelchair."

No weapon was found in the condo but after a re-examination of the place the police found a four-inch kitchen knife under the couch. The autopsy would reveal that the knife was the murder weapon. When this was revealed to Andrea she went and "prayed" and then would declare that she took the knife out of Sand's chest. She claimed she washed both the knife and her clothes.

Laster then asked Andrea if she were willing to take a lie detector test and she refused. At this point, he considered her to be the prime suspect.

The attack on Sand was brutal. The autopsy revealed that the fatal wounds had been to his aorta. He displayed defensive wounds on his arms and wounds which meant that he had been conscious and trying to ward off the attack. The autopsy physician surmised that Sand had been lying down when the attack took place.

PSYCHOTHERAPY

Andrea consulted with her therapist, Dr. Morton Kurland, and he told her to stop talking to the police and get an attorney. He recommended Gary Scherotter, considered the best criminal attorney in Palm Springs.

Andrea heeded his advice despite the fact it was quickly looking like she was a black widow on the prowl for a rich husband to kill.

A TURN FOR THE BIZARRE

On July 23rd, the Indio Sheriff's department received an emergency call from Andrea Sand's residence.

When police arrived they found Andrea nude on the kitchen floor. Her hands and feet were tied behind her and a knife was stuck in her buttocks.

She told the police that she had returned home after a visit to New Jersey. She stated that two men and a woman had tied her up and repeatedly raped her.

During the rape, the intruders informed her that they had murdered her husband and would be back for more.

"The police came into her home," Fanning said. "She was bound hand and foot. And she had a knife sticking out of her buttocks."

"We never found any evidence of the assault," Hawkins said. "We couldn't find any physical evidence on her."

Detective Chris Brown realized that the rope had been tied with slipknots and there was the possibility that Andrea had tied herself up. During an interview with Andrea, Brown stated that he doubted Andrea's story.

"If you don't believe me, why don't you arrest me?" Andrea challenged.

"It's possible you'll be arrested," Brown said. "Based on my past experience, one of three things is going to happen. You'll either kill yourself, kill someone else, or I'll have another call back here for another phony situation."

MORE "ATTACKS"

Andrea began calling the sheriffs on a regular basis, stating that the same intruders came and raped her again.

"She continued to tell us that the intruders returned, kidnapped and sexually assaulted her repeatedly. There were so many incidents."

She also produced numerous threatening letters which she claimed were from the gang of murderers/rapists.

The letters were determined to be fakes as the only fingerprints on the paper belonged to Andrea herself.

"I've been on the bench for fifteen years," Hawkins said. "And I haven't seen any cases as bizarre as this one.

"In all of her alleged attacks," Newsome said. "Andrea was always the victim. There was never any physical evidence or signs of forced entry. These were phantom intruders. She was tested for DNA and they found nothing. So the police knew that they were dealing with someone who was either schizophrenic or making the lamest attempt to throw them off her trail. Amazing that she had so little foresight into what she was doing. Like a bad screenwriter, she had no one to bounce her bizarre ideas off of so she ended up doing a lot of bizarre things that only tightened the noose around her own neck."

FINDING A NEW MAN

True to the pattern of her life, Andrea could not go long without a new man by her side. She would meet Joe Mack Mims at a Christmas party at the Evangelical Free Church. Mims was 56 years old, widowed and a water pump consultant.

Andrea had a neighbor who encouraged her to "find Jesus" and she came into the church of Mims who was a regular attendee of the services there.

Mims became enamored with Andrea and believed her stories about the murder of her ex-husband and the repeated attacks. He went so far as to visit the Deputy D.A. Jim Hawkins and complained that if they knew anything about police work they "would probably have the murderer by now."

Mims then informed Hawkins that he was going to marry Andrea. Hawkins advised Mims against this, stating that they were going to charge her with the murder of Sand.

"Go ahead and charge her," Mims replied. "I'm still going to marry her."

"He became irate," Hawkins said. "He suggested that I spend my time trying to find the intruders that keep returning and assaulting her. And stop harassing her."

"Mims had a classic case of 'Captain Save-A-Ho,'" Newsome said. "Here was this woman who has worked as a call-girl, has two children, has been married five times and he is naïve enough to believe that after listening to a few sermons she is a changed woman. So he becomes her savior, marches down to the police station to intimidate them, marches down to the D. A's office. All the while, Andrea is not saying a word. She has a new man to do her bidding, to plead her case. She's damn good at finding these kind of men. She had been doing it her whole life."

FIRST DEGREE MURDER CHARGES

On March 25th, 1982, Andrea's attorney Gary Scherotter was notified by the D.A.'s office that Andrea would be charged with first degree murder. Scherotter sent her to the court where she posted $100,000 bail and was set free.

The next day, Andrea and Joe Mims were married.

SIXTH TIME IS A CHARM?

Andrea did not want to sell the condo at The Springs until Sand's estate was settled. Mims sold his own home and moved in with Andrea at The Springs.

"He took it upon himself to try and protect her from the return of the intruders who kept kidnapping and assaulting her," Hawkins said.

"Again, the poor guy is smitten by her charms," Newsome said. "Here is a 56-year old man living as an anonymous life as possible. He meets a woman sixteen years his junior. She's stunning, she's posed in Playboy, been in movies and now she is reformed at the church of his choice. He's convinced she's in love with him and is willing to move heaven and earth to make protect that illusion."

MORE BIZARRE STUNTS

Two months later after they were married, however, Mims called the police and informed them that Andrea had been kidnapped. The officers began a search but Andrea returned home on the same day claiming she had been abducted and raped by the same intruders as before.

No physical evidence was found but Mims remained steadfast in his belief that Andrea was telling the truth.

Andrea was able to put on a false front with Mims, appearing to genuinely care about the man as they would engage in social gatherings at church.

But on Halloween of 1982, Andrea convinced Mims that they should take a drive together. They drove along Highway 74 and turned into an isolated dirt road. Andrea threw a bed sheet on the gravel and began to give Mims fellatio.

Mims climaxed into her mouth after which she spit his semen into a tissue. She then told him to roll over on his stomach and she would give him a massage.

"So Joe thinks this is the best thing going," Fanning said

Mims was like putty under her expert hands but then something hit him hard on the back of the head.

He screamed in pain until he was hit again.

Turning around, he saw Andrea holding a hammer, wanting to hit him again. He pushed her off and grabbed her arm, ripping the hammer out of her grip.

"What in the name of God are you doing?" he asked.

"I've got to knock you out so that people will believe I've been raped."

Mims finally saw the light. He knew that she had thought to use the semen in the tissue to provide evidence she had been raped.

"The fact that she tried to kill him (Mims) was a real game changer," Hawkins said. "The evidence that we needed to really go forward on the case."

KNOCKED INTO COMING INTO HIS SENSES

Mims dressed and drove Andrea home before going to the hospital to get his head stitched up.

The next morning, Mims moved out of the condo. He notified authorities of the assault, prompting an attempted murder charge to be added to the first degree case against Andrea.

Mims moved to have his marriage with Andrea annulled. Andrea's bail was then revoked and she went to jail to await the trial.

Andrea's attorney, Gary Scherotter, now believed that she wasn't mentally stable and had the court examine her for competency. Andrea was taken to Riverside General Hospital for observation and tried to commit suicide twice during her stay there by slashing her wrists.

"Her whole world finally came crashing down," Newsome said. "She was completely out of control. A psychologically broken woman with no way out and no answers, she finally broke down and tried to end it all."

MENTALLY COMPETENT

Scherotter would resign as her attorney as the Sand estate had been tied up in litigation and she could no longer afford to pay him. Andrea was appointed a public defender in Charles Stafford who changed Andrea's please from not guilty to not guilty by reason of insanity. His defense lay in the hopes that the jury would believe that Andrea had been driven crazy by the men in her life who abused her and it all came to a blowout when Robert Sand forced her to be the victim in his bizarre, sadomasochistic fantasies.

But the prosecution found a man named Richard Cordine who was a convict serving a twelve year sentence for robbery at a Nevada State Prison. Cordine stated that Andrea had started a pen pal relationship with him in 1977 which continued for years until Joe Mims found out about it and stopped it. Cordine would testify that Andrea called him after the Sand murder and confessed "I stabbed the bastard."

Her prosecutor, Robert Dunn, would call her a "malingerer who would lie to achieve her own end." He dismissed the idea of Andrea killing Sand out of self-defense on the grounds that Robert was a paraplegic.

"She planned Sand's murder to get money from his will," Dunn said. "She received about $150,000 in cash and $100,000 equity in the couple's condominium."

"She stabbed the man twenty-seven times," Newsome said. "This scared the crap out of the jurors. Andrea would take the stand and give the performance of her life by recounting her tales of abuse but in the end, it was those twenty-seven stab wounds that stayed in the mind of the jurors."

After deliberation, a ten-woman, two man jury found Andrea Mims guilty of first degree murder. The judge sentenced her to 26 years to life and sent her to the California Institute for Women in Frontera.

"When the judge read the verdict to her," Fanning said. "She slammed down a box of tissues on the thing (table) and said 'I killed him because he called me a whore!'"

"Manipulation always worked for Andrea," Newsome said. "She knew how to manipulate men all her life. She thought she could manipulate everyone else the same way, cops, jurors, telling them about her tales of abuse and woe and thereby mitigating her own culpability in all the bad things she did.

REMARRIAGE?

Joe Mims tried to jump start his life after Andrea was sentenced but could not seem to get over her. He knew that she had killed Robert Sand but also believed she had been forced to do it as her attorney had claimed. He then heard a radio program discussing PMS and concluded that Andrea had suffered from the condition when she killed her husband and attacked him.

Mims did research on PMS then visited Andrea in prison, telling her of his findings. Andrea requested progesterone from the jailhouse doctor but the physician found no symptoms of PMS. He finally gave in to her demands, however, and the drug seemed to improve her demeanor.

Andrea displayed good behavior in prison. Mims had a renewed hope that he would get a new trial for Andrea on the basis of his PMS theory. He proposed marriage once again and Andrea accepted. He wrote love letters to Andrea such as the one below:

"My Darling Drea,

I promise you a love that will be true, I will always put you first in my life. I will do all I can to meet your every need, while we are apart it will be hard, but our God will bring you home to me. I love you with all my heart,

Your Hubby,

Joe"

On May 13th, 1986, Mims showed up at the prison to marry Andrea. He never made it past the front gate, however, as he began to experience chest pain then collapse. He was transported to to Chino Community Hospital where he was pronounced dead of a heart attack.

After Mims' death, Andrea once again reiterated her story that intruders had killed Robert Sand.

During her prison term she became a prolific artist at the Central California Women's facility and won several awards as well as becoming a Buddhist.

"I'm very proud of my achievements," she said in a prison newsletter. "I've used the past 20 plus years to improve myself, learning to grow in a positive way and also to heal and forgive myself."

Andrea was paroled in 2012 but suffered from ovarian cancer which soon got into her lungs. She would die at the Mesa Verde Convalescent Hospital in Costa Mesa, CA.

"I do understand that she suffered at the hands of men," Hawkins said. "Why she had the relationship problems that she did but I don't think that was ever an excuse to forgive or forget what she did to Robert Sand."

AMNESIAC KILLER : THE TRUE STORY OF DANIELLE STEWART

LES ACKERMAN

"I would punish all of those who had never lost anything, those who had never had anything taken away from them. I would let the anger from my chest reach out and explode in spectacular violence." - An excerpt from a poem by Danielle Stewart

Danielle Stewart had a normal and happy childhood until around the age of seven. Both of her parents were public servants and the family lived in the Curtin, Canberra region of Australia. She had one younger sister and the family seemed en route to living a normal, happy life.

Danielle was particularly close to her father during her childhood years. He took her swimming, read books to her at night and sang to her. She described him as being a man with a great sense of humor and the kind of man who "did all the things that dads do."

At the age of seven, however, Danielle's life took a traumatic turn. Her family was building a holiday house in the NSW south coast town of Batemans Bay. Danielle, unfortunately, came into the cross hairs of a sexual predator.

The man was a neighbor and Danielle would come over to his home to watch TV as they had no television of their own in their holiday house. The man was a married real estate agent in his 50s. He would let Danielle and a friend come with him to outings where they would examine unoccupied houses he was selling. It was there, inside these homes, that the assaults would take place.

Danielle would be under the man's spell for over three years before they molestations came to an end.

When she was eleven years old, tragedy struck again in the form of losing her mother to cancer. Distraught, her father sent her away for a weekend with a friend of a family. The family had a teenaged son, however, who constantly harassed Danielle, molesting her as well.

Her father would remarry six months later to a woman who had three children of her own. Danielle felt betrayed by her father's remarriage and tried to commit suicide with an overdose of pills. Her father himself had suffered from depression and fell apart emotionally after the death of Danielle's mother.

"I've always believed that depression and mental illness is inheritable," forensic psychologist Pauline Malloy said. "Sometimes through genetics, sometimes through thought processes. With Danielle, she clearly inherited some mental illness from her father's side of the family as her dad suffered from depression as well as her paternal grandfather."

Her maternal grandparents arrived and offered that Danielle come live with them. Danielle didn't want to go, she wanted to stay with her Dad but her father didn't want her screwing up the dynamics of his new family with her bad behavior.

He wanted her gone.

So Danielle was given two choices, either go live with her grandparents or go to a youth shelter.

Danielle chose to run away

"Danielle suffered numerous traumas, back to back," Malloy said. "The loss of her innocence, the loss of her mom and then the rejection of her father. Any of the above could have been cause for life altering psychological trauma but she suffered all of these within a four year time span. It had to crush her psychically and she did not have the life experience to cope."

Running away, the twelve year old girl roughed it out on the streets. Finally, she grew tired and returned home to her father. She would not be treated as the prodigal daughter, however, as her father had her bags packed and waiting. He drove Danielle to a local youth shelter and dropped her off.

Danielle would remain there for the next three months.

Danielle did not like the youth refuge. There was a lot of drug use, alcohol and she once again experienced sexual abuse.

"This was a horrid life for her at this point," Malloy said. "At some point I think she broke down psychologically and the seeds for future violent behavior were planted here."

RETURNING HOME

She eventually returned home to live with her father but he had settled in with his new family.

"I felt so alone, unloved, misunderstood," Danielle recalled. "and as the problems at home got worse, I got worse. I was sneaking out of the house, drinking, drugging. I missed my mum so terribly, I just wanted to be with her."

Danielle would attempt suicide on several occasions, leaving permanent scars on her wrist.

"I used a razor in my bedroom downstairs," Danielle said. "There was no internet back then and I didn't know how to do it [properly]."

On her 13th birthday, her father celebrated by throwing her out of the house once again. She would go and live with her friend Elle O'Brien and her mother. O'Brien's mother fed her and took her in, allowing the unwanted girl to remain there for four years.

At the age of sixteen, she enrolled at Narrabundah College and become a student of renowned poet Geoff Page.

"She was leagues ahead of anyone I've encountered writing contemporary poetry at that age," Page recalled. "She had some of the same virtues as Sylvia Plath, a real feeling for adventurous imagery. There was a lot going on in her brain at an intense level and she had the talent to turn it into something moving."

Under the guidance of her teacher, Danielle published an anthology of poems called "I for Icarus."

Danielle would go on to study performing arts at Melbourne's Monash University before traveling to Sydney to share an apartment with her step-sister, Myfanwy Thompson. Both young women would indulge in alcohol and prescription drugs, becoming the catalyst for each others self-destructive behavior. Myfanwy, however, would suffer a freak accident in falling off a cliff while taking ecstasy.

The loss devastated Danielle as she considered Myfanwy to be her best friend.

"Her boyfriend had got into dealing ecstasy," Danielle said. "I couldn't handle seeing her wasted all the time, so I'd moved out with other friends."

Her younger step-brother, Tristram would later die of an aneurysm after being diagnosed with schizophrenia.

MEANDERING THROUGH LIFE

Danielle was now 24 and wandered aimlessly through life. She went from one job to the next until she met the 50-year old Chaim Kimel in late 2000.

"They met on the dance floor and hit it off immediately," journalist Byron Kaye said.

Despite the age difference, Chaim Kamel was a stylish man with his own business.

"He was a bit of a bon vivant," crime author Paul Kidd said. "Lived in the good part of Sydney. A good lifestyle."

"He was very charismatic, very gregarious, very charming, very generous, strong and creative," Danielle said. "He loved his children and they loved him."

Kimel had been a successful entrepreneur, dealing in antiques. She got a job working for Chaim in his furniture store, Eclectica in Mosman. Kimel had put Danielle in charge of bookkeeping.

The two got along exceptionally well, at first, with common interests in art, music, and food.

"Danielle was a very attractive," Kidd said. "Petite, blonde, loved to drink. He (Chaim) was an older man but a really good style of a bloke."

The relationship started platonic in the beginning.

"He made some advances which weren't initially reciprocated," Kaye said. "But over time, they became intimate and it was on."

Kimel thought Danielle was a "prize catch". He invited Danielle over to visit his family and she was impressed with how close and living they were. There she saw, for the first time since her early childhood, a loving family that she could be a part of.

Danielle moved in with Kimel who had the time lived with his ten year old son Jordan. He also had a daughter, Amber and Fred, who were in their early twenties and late teens respectively.

A CHANGE IN DEMEANOR?

One of her friends, however, thought that Danielle changed after she met Chaim. She described him as being very possessive and told her what to do.

"I loved him," Danielle said. "I still do. It is a love-hate thing and it won't ever go. With those types of personalities, there is that level of attention, you become their entire focus."

Danielle would have these kind of intense relationships all of her life and it seemed to be the fuel to her fire. She was irresistibly drawn to the drama and would have it on full blast with Chaim Kimel.

"Anyone who would have been in a relationship with Danielle Stewart would have been in a relationship that was doomed from the start," Kidd said. "The combination of psychological problems fueled by excesses of alcohol was always going to end in disaster."

COCAINE AND BOOZE

Danielle began substance abuse at an early age which only progressed as she got older. She now had a benefactor in Chaim as well as an enabler as he liked to party, indulging in cocaine himself.. He didn't realize, however, that the alcohol would only stoke the flames that would extinguish their relationship.

He also had a dark side, according to Danielle's grandmother. She described him as someone who was "demanding and overpowering."

"She (Danielle) went through life with a paranoia that people were going to leave her," Kidd said. "And she became very, very possessive of her partner and that fueled by alcohol was the basis of the majority of their problems."

CALL THE POLICE

Once the relationship turned intimate, things started getting out of hand. The two indulged in alcohol and had numerous fights in which the police were called in.

Danielle had been taking strong anti-depression medications and mixing these drugs with alcohol. One fight had gotten so severe that she took a restraining order out against Kimel.

On one occasion, Kimel violated the order and was jailed for one night.

"I'd moved into temporary accommodation and Chaim came after me," Danielle said. "He broke into my room and stole my laptop and wallet. The police busted him on the way out and took him to jail for the night."

Kimel explained to the police that he violated the order because Danielle had called him stating that she had swallowed fourteen Valiums.

"I'm fine when I'm not in an emotional situation," Danielle said, "but when I'm under threat, the flashbacks can be extreme."

"She (Danielle) had a borderline personality disorder," Malloy said. "When things go bad with her, they go real bad. That was how she lived her entire life up until that point. She had to engage in fights, drinking, drugs. Drama, drama, drama. If it isn't there, she will create it."

A PROPENSITY FOR VIOLENCE

Kimel's son, Jordan, was ten years old when his father first met Danielle. He recalled Danielle as a destructive psychotic stating that she would "cut up $10,000 worth of business suits, delete important documents from my father's computer. Once, she punched through a glass bathroom window and slashed her wrists. And she'd punch my father, too."

"Unfortunately, this was the pattern that was set," Malloy set. "They would argue, fight and then get back together. When they would get back together things would be more passionate and clingy than before. 'Please, don't leave me,' that sort of thing. But then the cycle repeats itself and it has to be more extreme in order for the couple to get that same 'high.'"

The couple would remain together and make attempts to appear respectable. In 2004, Danielle enrolled at a nearby college to finish her degree while they both started an online catering company called Epicurean. The money to start the company was borrowed from Danielle's grandmother, a total of $30,000.

Later that year, the couple would journey to India where they would marry at the Taj Mahal.

Danielle would claim, however, that the money the borrowed for the business is what kept her in the marriage .

"Part of the reason I married Chaim was because I was worried about my grandparents' money," Danielle said. "If I left him, there'd be no legal recourse for me to get it back. He took it without shame; he never planned to pay it back."

"Typical of people with borderline personality disorders," Malloy said. "Is that they have to play the role of the victim. It is a head scratcher as to why Chaim would borrow thirty-grand when he had his own business. Maybe he thought he would be placating her somehow with them being in business together and having her feel as if she were a part of things. But clearly he didn't need anything more on his plate."

BOOMERANG BABY

Danielle would leave Kimel a total of seven times during their seven year relationship. She would confide in her grandmother and friend Elle, saying she was unhappy. Then he would call and they would get back together.

"It (their relationship) was very alcohol fueled," Kaye said. "Very hedonistic. A lot of violent arguments."

Danielle blamed her inability to stay away from Chaim on her lack of self-esteem.

"While he could be caring, it was undermined by his desire to keep me enslaved to him," Danielle said. "When I left him, he'd follow me and get me back. When your sense of self-esteem is so low and a learnt helplessness has set in, you don't feel able to support yourself. My friends had dropped off because they couldn't stand him. The only times I responded with violence were when I was trying to leave and he'd try to stop me. He'd hide my wallet, phone, computer, passport. Those times always ended with me being in hospital, not him. I never tried to kill him: I tried to kill myself."

WHO WAS ABUSING WHO?

It became apparent to Kimel's family, however, that he had married a woman prone to violent outbursts. Kimel told his daughter than Danielle had bitten him on his thumb and arm as as smashing his glasses.

He had his glasses broken so much that it had become a "running joke", according to his daughter Amber.

After arguments, Danielle would delete Kimel's emails and computer files. Kimel had became so enraged at her actions that he kicked her out of the house. Danielle would return, kicking out the timber door.

WELCOME TO THE PSYCH WARD

Danielle had overdosed on medication numerous times during the course of her marriage. She would inform doctors that Kimel was controlling and that she had "nothing to live for."

His daughter, Amber, however, expressed concern for her father's well being and wanted him to sever ties with Danielle.

"He told me he'd made a commitment to be there for her and loved her unconditionally," Amber said. "He was convinced unconditional love would cure her."

"Chaim was the rescuer," Malloy said. "He couldn't help himself. Danielle was the beautiful damsel in distress. They had passionate sex together, he knew about her past, and he couldn't be another man that brought more pain in her life. He didn't want that. He thought that through his own sincerity and love that he could somehow bring her to a place of healing. But he wasn't a professional. And that isn't what relationships are for."

A NEW MAN

In 2006, Danielle separated from Kimel and met Melbourne university professor Joeri Mol. She moved in with him and became pregnant by December of that year. Danielle wanted to go back to Sydney, however, and didn't want to raise the child with Mol as a single mother.

"She went out with somebody else," Kaye said. "He was seeing other people but they could not stop speaking. They remained extremely close. The new fellow (Mol) wants to settle down and start raising a family. Which incidentally was Danielle's greatest dream, which was to have a family. But she's still drawn to Chaim uncontrollably."

A week later, she called Kimel and the two met to discuss a reconciliation.

"He (Chaim) told her that either she as a termination," Kidd said. "Or there's no hope if them ever getting back together."

She complied with his request, her second abortion in six months (the first with Kimel) and she once again went into a depression.

"Danielle desperately wanted to experience the happiness that she had before her mother died," Malloy said. "She always told her grandmother, 'I just want have a normal life. I just want to have a normal life.' What she really wanted was that family again. So now she spends her life grasping at straws, going from this man to that man, and getting multiple abortions."

BURNING THE CANDLE AT BOTH ENDS

The couple moved back in together in 2007 but this time their break-up would be much more volatile.

And violent.

"It was short lived (their reconciliation)," Kidd said. "Now that they were back together. It was business as usual."

Business as usual was a lot of fighting and alcohol coupled with a flurry of activity to keep up with the bills.

Danielle returned to college and continued to run their catering business, The Epicurean. In order to make ends meet, however, she took a part time job at a Sydney ad agency.

She couldn't juggle all of these things at once, so she turned to cocaine and alcohol. Her friends described her as "withdrawn" and "unsettled" after meeting with her after the latest reconciliation.

Danielle began to feel the itch to run away again, telling friends she now just wanted to earn some money on her own and get away from Kimel for good.

"How the hell could this have worked to begin with?" Malloy said. "You've got a woman with some serious issues, abused by men, abandoned as a child and now she's an alcoholic with major depression. The pattern is set in their relationship. Break-up, get back together, fight some more. Rinse and repeat. This can only end badly. The question was, how bad?"

THE FATEFUL DINNER

"The old problems kept resurfacing," Kaye said. "They kept on with the dinner parties. Living the good life. And with this came Danielle's terrible response to alcohol access."

On August 23rd of 2007, Danielle went out with Kimel to have dinner at a restaurant called Pescador. They were described in a police statement by their friend, Angela Batley, to be in "good spirits."

"It is noted by others there that Danielle seemed a little drunker than usual," Kaye said. "Things got a little bit more testy and Danielle left and decided to walk home."

After dinner, Chaim went with his friends to Angela Batley's home. He would call Danielle from the home and she said that she would come and pick him up. Things took a turn for the strange when Danielle came over but drove back without Chaim who ended up walking home.

Batley was concerned about the tenseness of the situation and called Kimel to make sure he got home safe. Kimel told Batley that Danielle was working on the computer but was "drunk" and that he had to go.

Danielle arrived at their home before Kimel. She told the 16-year old Jordan that she "shouldn't have gone to Angela's house. I've had too much to drink."

Jordan stated that Danielle began playing loud music through the computer, dancing with a drink in her hand. When Kimel arrived, he told her to turn the music down before the neighbors start complaining. An argument ensued before Kimel turned off Danielle's music himself. The argument escalated, the topics being the loud music then escalating to the fact that Chaim would change the password on the computer, which was an ongoing issue in their relationship.

She started to physically attack him but Chaim easily evaded the rushes of the drunk Danielle. Then in the heat of the moment, she picked up one of Chaim's antique ornamental knives he had on display. Chaim came forward, ordering her to place the knife down, then she stuck it into his stomach.

Chaim fell to the ground and she stabbed him again.

"They were both yelling for about 15 minutes," stated Jordan. "All of a sudden, I could hear them in the corridor outside my room. It sounded like someone was being hit or punched and I heard my father say, 'Why are you being violent and attacking me?' They kept fighting and I heard Danielle fall to the floor and scream. Soon after this, I heard my father say in a tense voice, 'What are you doing? Are you crazy?' I heard my father scream three times. I saw [his] white shirt was covered in blood all up the left side from underneath his ribs towards the middle of his torso. Danielle was standing about two metres away and she had our antique knife in her hand."

Jordan saw his father struggling to get to the front door. He was covered in blood and Danielle was hysterical, holding up the knife.

"So the son runs out of his room," Kaye said. "He finds his father clutching his stomach where he's been stabbed twice. Covered in blood. Barely able to speak."

Jordan then thought about attacking Danielle himself.

"He picks up a golf club then thinks for a moment, that he might avenge his father," Kaye said. "It's actually Chaim himself who tells him don't do it. Lying there, sort of holding himself together. The son puts the golf club down and nurses his father while he lies there dying."

Kimel would be rushed to the hospital but die on the operating table at St. Vincent's Hospital, bleeding to death from the two stab wounds to his stomach.

"To the end of his life," Malloy said. "Kimel was protecting Danielle. When his son wanted revenge, he held him back."

Danielle was arrested but plead not guilty on the grounds of self defense. Her blood alcohol reading, however, was five times the legal driving limit.

"It was a stupid, pointless, uncontrolled lover's argument," Kaye said. "And one split second decision led to this terrible outcome."

Danielle maintained no recollection of the events, as she mixed the anti-psychotic drug Seroquel with alcohol. She awoke in a prison cell and called out for her husband, seeing her name on the board with the word 'Murder' written next to it.

"It was the worst moment of my life," Danielle recalled. "In one instant, my entire life had changed and Chaim's had ended."

"Something was going to happen that night," Malloy said. "Her mind was on edge. This may not have been pre-meditated but she knew what was going to happen when she picked up that knife. Remember, she didn't just slash at him as a warning. She thrust the knife into Chaim. Not once. But twice. There was an untapped rage there that came to the surface at the moment. It had been bubbling for a long, long time and unfortunately Chaim Kimel could not foresee how this would end."

THE AFTERMATH

Danielle made a recorded phone call to her father a few days after the killing.

"If I could swap Chaim with me right now, I would do it immediately," Danielle said. "There is no way I meant to kill him."

"Again, I don't think the murder was pre-planned," Malloy said. "But it did seem to be part of Danielle's destiny. What we see here in her killing of Chaim was a metaphor of her own trauma. She was abused by a man in his fifties, molested by him from the ages of seven through ten. She grows into a beautiful woman can choose just about whatever man she wants but instead she elects a man in his fifties, over twenty-five years her senior. That is no coincidence. She is repeating her trauma from the past. But this time she wants to control it. She wants to exorcise the demons of the past so all of those violent fights are trial runs until finally she reaches for that knife and stabs Chaim, metaphorically killing the molester of her past. Now her husband, who actually really loved her, is the victim of this cycle of abuse that has finally come full circle."

Her father agreed to post Danielle's bail but would not agree to the 24-hour surveillance condition attached to it. Her father abandoning her yet again, she turned to her friend Elle O'Brien's mother. She came to bail out Danielle and secured her release after nine months.

Danielle then went to live with her grandmother.

Facing twenty-five years in prison, Danielle would attempt suicide two more times, one of them involving an overdose of Seroquel.

"When I took that Seroquel, I went into psychosis," Danielle said. "It was an out-of-body experience where I thought the nurses were talking about me even though they weren't. I was watching myself from afar. It was crazy, crazy shit. I am sure that is what must have happened on the night Chaim died."

"The psych med plus alcohol defense has become a cliched defense for a lot of killers," Malloy said. "Danielle had done her research. She had studied scriptwriting in school. Everything she said and did had a rehearsed feel to it."

FROM MURDER TO MANSLAUGHTER

The murder charge had been downgraded to manslaughter as Danielle maintained she had no recollection of what happened. She did not remember any of the events of what happened that night not to mention taking the ornamental knife and stabbing her husband with it.

She did not take the stand, however.

"Danielle was charged with murder," Kaye said. "She wept throughout much of the trial. It was very clear that she regretted what she'd done and she wanted him back and she felt quite horrible."

Kimel's children, however, saw Danielle as an imposter the more they investigated the case. They found a synopsis of a play that Danielle had been working on. In the story, one of the characters had a secret desire to kill her older husband.

Fred Kimel, Chaim's oldest son, noted that the play contained details on "jail architecture, prisoner psychology, different cell classifications, prisoner attire, prison visiting hours and life sentences."

The Kimel family once enamored with Danielle, now saw her in a completely different light.

"It was a university assignment, a book I was writing," Danielle said. "I heard that somewhere men kill their partners because they want them to stay, whereas women kill their partners because they want to escape. I know why I was writing about prison: because I was imprisoned long before I was [actually] incarcerated."

SENTENCING

Danielle would be sentenced to six years in prison. She would serve only four.

"There's no doubt that jail saved me," Danielle said. "It prevented me from harming myself with alcohol and drugs. I wouldn't recommend it, though."

During the first nine months of her term, she had been housed in the mental health unit. She could not stop crying. But the prison assigned her to a job in the kitchen and she found her fellow inmates to be helpful.

"I managed to get a few of the heavies on side somehow and avoided the others where possible," Danielle said. "I learnt to assimilate, to hide the fact that I was pretty and educated. I adapted where I could. In jail, I lost everything that made me me: my family, dog, business, house, studies, friends, freedom, clothes, make-up, choices. All I had was myself, my mind and my heart. I learnt to spot evil from a mile away - and evil does exist, I've come face to face with it - but I could still love. This is how I got through jail. Yes, I learnt how to operate within the system, but I could still see beauty in people, and I tried to speak to that."

"Danielle was a well-spoken, educated young woman," Malloy said. "But why the hell would she plead not guilty? She did her research on prison culture beforehand so a cynic can argue that she got off very, very light for what she did. Call it misandry, call it getting the female pass, Danielle was able to get off light for a cold-blooded murderer. She used all of the things from her past to mitigate her own culpability. Sexual abuse, parental death and abandonment down to psych meds and alcohol. She combined those things to get sympathy from Chaim and later from the her jury of her crime."

Danielle walked out of prison on June 24th, 2010.

She is now focused on the prospect of moving to Spain and becoming a professional writer.

"I've paid for what has happened and I've done all I can to fix the issues within myself that contributed to Chaim's death," Danielle said. "I see both a psychiatrist and a psychologist, both of my own volition, nothing to do with parole directives. I don't drink. I don't take drugs. I take responsibility for my actions. I write when I can. I try to love my friends and family. I try to see beauty in the world and I'd like to hope, one day, that I can contribute to that beauty. Still, I love. I still love Chaim. I still love my father. In the end, love will be all I have."

TWISTED SISTERS : THE TRUE STORY OF REGINA AND MARGARET DEFRANCISCO

KORI MAYER

CHAPTER ONE

Regina and Margaret DeFrancisco are two sisters convicted of first degree murder.

On paper, the two sisters look like two girls you would see at a church social.

In school, both were good but not great students. Margaret was the pretty one. She would get all of the attention from the boys but return little interest.

Margaret was a student at Jones College Prep School, a selective public institution that is considered one of the top high schools in Illinois.

A little on the shy side, Margaret had a quick wit and sense of humor. Sweet-looking and pretty, she had avoided any kind of trouble throughout her young life. Her early photos suggest, however, that her subtle smirk was a couldn't contain the narcissism that was growing within.

"You would look at Margaret and see right through her," one of her neighbors said. "It was black, like was nothing there. She didn't seem like she had depth, like she had compassion."

Regina had a love for animals, particularly ponies. She rode horses and in her words, "never lost a show."

Regina was also the more extroverted of the two, wearing her emotions on her sleeve. She could mouth off and had a chip on her shoulder. She also had a thing for 'bad boys', seeing them as a reflection of herself.

"A lot of girls get turned on by the 'thug life'," forensic psychologist Marnie Clark said. "The DeFrancisco sisters definitely fit that mold. They were not out to play Mrs. Cleaver when they grew up. They were attracted to the gang lifestyle. They thought the drama was exciting."

The girls were raised by a single parent, Nora DeFrancisco. Nora raised the two sisters and their brother Joey in the Pilsen neighborhood of Chicago. Their father, Augie DeFrancisco was a small-time burglar and convicted drug dealer who had no involvement in the girl's childhood years. Their maternal grandfather, Gilbert Smith, was a former Chicago cop who was fired from the force in 1960 after admitting that he was "friendly with certain burglars."

Growing up in Pilsen, however, the girls could not avoid rubbing shoulders with gang members. They became enamored with gang culture, learning who fought against who and what the names of the gangs were. There were the Latin Counts, Kool Gang, Villa Lobos, Bishops, among many other offshoots. The girls knew what streets signified what gang members' territory and memorized their hand signals.

"Chicago is simply rife with gangs," Clark said. "It is inescapable, even to those in the more affluent communities. There is still a choice, however. For whatever reason, the DeFrancisco sisters were drawn to the 'thug life'. To a young person, it looks 'cool'. They are the classic examples of young women who could not see the big picture and thought the thug life was something worth aspiring to."

The two sisters, with their striking brunette looks, could not help but come into the cross hairs of the local gang members. They began wearing dark lipstick and teasing their hair out. Margaret would get a tattoo on her belly. Regina would have the letter "R" tattooed on her leg as well as a drawing of a heart just above her breast. They would hang out on street corners and in front of the local liquor store, chatting up the neighborhood 'gangstas'.

"The changes in their make-up and dress signified the changes in their personality," Clark said. "They grew bored during their time at prep school. Even ashamed. They did not want to see themselves as nerds and hated that aspect of themselves. Starting in eighth grade, it was time to start rebelling. By the time they reached high-school, the thug life was part of their persona. Dark make-up. Tattoos. Hanging out with gang bangers. Alcohol and drugs. But most important, they wanted all the drama that came with that kind of life. Who is out to get who, who dissed who and who shot who became their modus operandi in life."

Grandfather Gilbert, however, had seen this all before as a Chicago cop. He feared that the girls, particularly Regina, would become ensnared by the street gang culture. He tried to obstruct this from happening and found Regina a job with a local periodontist. He figured if he kept the girl busy with school and work it would keep her away from the idiots on the street.

Regina, however, did not have the emotional maturity to see the light. She showed up late for her first couple of shifts then she was fired.

But she had started dating a man named Johnny Rivera, a known member of Chicago's notorious "Latin Kings" street gang. Rivera had a rap sheet as long as "War and Peace" as well as more aliases than a Russian spy

Regina would learn how to package and deal drugs at the foot of Johnny. She would watch him put the cocaine into plastic bags, measuring it out by the ounce. They would drive around town and Johnny would introduce her to his customers, watching as he conducted the deals. The secret handshakes and secret lingo all became apart of Regina's world.

Officially crossing over from innocent prep school girl to drug dealing girlfriend, Regina lived a double life. She did manage to get a part-time job doing data entry work for a local law firm and had enrolled in the local junior college (Harold Washington).

Margaret was getting into trouble as well. Her grades in high school were slipping as she would sneak out at night to be with friends. She would often come to school looking "disheveled" according to one teacher who thought she looked like a child whose parents were going through a divorce.

And there was trouble on the home front.

Neighbors would report hearing the girls fighting with their mother on a daily basis.. The two girls were out of control with no father figure to put them in line. Nora would berate Regina whenever she would act up in school or get arrested and the girls would yell back.

In private, Nora would refer to her daughters as "the bitches".

Things would come to a head when Regina would get arrested for selling cocaine to an undercover cop. A single mom already strapped for cash as she had to support three children on her own, Nora was livid as she paid Regina's bail.

"How are you going to pay me back?" .

"I don't know!"

"Do you know how much it costs to bail you out of jail!" Nora screamed. "You are going to pay me back. You're going to pay me back every penny!"

CHAPTER TWO

"She needs money," Margaret said, her voice full of concern.

"How much?" Oscar asked.

"One thousand dollars. Can you help us out, baby?"

That was the scene set for the twenty-two year old Oscar Velazquez in June of 2000 as he spoke to the sister of his current teenage crush, Regina DeFrancisco. He spotted Regina around the neighborhood of Pilsen and quickly fell for her dark Irish-Italian good looks. Showing off his brand new Z28 Camaro, he chatted up the girls before he asked Regina out for tacos. The two began going out but Regina didn't like him...at first. Then she realized that he had some money and was all too willing to spend it on her.

"Oscar wasn't the typical guy that Regina would go for," Clark said. "Regina liked the 'bad boy', the thug. Oscar wasn't in street gang culture. He had immigrated from Mexico and actually had a real job, earning his living the old fashioned way as a truck driver. If anything, Regina would see someone like him as a sucker, someone who she could use."

Still, Regina was what Oscar wanted. He persisted in calling her, asking when he could see her again.

"He's a creepy guy," Regina told her sister, Margaret as her cell phone rang. She looked at the caller ID. Yep, it was Oscar.

"But maybe you can get some money from him?"

"Here, you talk to him," Regina said handing the cell phone to Margaret. "Just make up some baloney that I'm in jail or something."

"What?"

"Get rid of him. Tell him I need bail money."

"Hello, Oscar?" Margaret answered the phone.

"Yeah," Oscar said. "Who is this?"

"It's Margaret," she said, sounding as if she was trying to stifle tears. "Regina is in jail. She's locked up."

"What?"

"They put her in jail for something she didn't even do. They want one thousand dollars. One thousand dollars to bail her out."

Margaret smiled like a devil at her sister.

"I can help," Oscar said.

"No," Margaret said, sniffling. "It's too much."

"It's for your sister."

Oscar would persist in his willingness to help out, however. Margaret played him like a violin, agreeing to meet with Oscar to take his hard earned money.

"Oscar gave Margaret the money in the hopes of scoring points with the sisters," Clark said. "He thought that by being 'nice' and bailing them out of trouble they would find him attractive. Instead, it just fueled their contempt for him. These girls liked thugs. Bums. They cared little for Oscar's chivalry."

Regina would not use the money to pay back her mother, however. She would give the money to her real boyfriend, Johnny, who bought an "old school ride" car with Oscar's money.

Oscar would call Regina over twenty-four times during the next five days wanting to know what happened. He began to feel like the sucker he was.

He had a wife and kids in Mexico. But here in Chicago he fell for the brown-haired beauty and became all too willing to be her patsy.

"Oscar was playing with fire," Clark said. "He just didn't realize how far gone the girls were in terms of narcissism. He didn't see the fact that they didn't even see him as a human being. All he saw was batting eyelashes and pretty faces. He was totally smitten with Regina despite the fact that he had a wife and kids back in Mexico. Here he was, in Chicago, where he was free from the responsibilities of family. He could have a little fun and if he had to spend some money to do it, so be it."

CHAPTER THREE

The two sisters were surprised at how easy it was to extract money out of Oscar. With one fake phone call, they had one thousand dollars cash to their name.

"They were both attractive girls in the neighborhood," Clark said. "They were young, looking up to gang members and drug dealers for the power they had. But the girls realized that they had their own power. The power of budding sexuality that could make men do what they wanted. They could trick men into doing things for them with a future promise of sex."

Oscar continued to call and it would be only a matter of time before he would be confronted with the truth that he had been lied to. The girls had to construct a plan to get rid of him.

"I have an idea," Margaret said, picking up the cell phone and calling their fifteen year old friend, Veronica Garcia.

"Need your help," Margaret said as Veronica picked up.

"For what?" Veronica asked.

"I need a gun. Can you get a gun?"

"A gun?"

"Can your boyfriend get a gun?"

Veronica, like the DeFrancisco sisters, was enamored with street gang members. She had a boyfriend who could obtain whatever you needed, drugs or guns.

"Why?"

"We're going to stick up and rob Oscar," she said.

"You're not going to kill him are you?"

"We're just going to scare him a little," Margaret laughed.

Veronica did as she was asked, getting a gun from her boyfriend and heading straight over to the DeFrancisco sister's home.

"Nice," Margaret said, looking the pistol over, closing one eye as she looked through the cross hairs. "So where we going to do this?"

"Right here," Regina said, waving her hands around the living room.

"No way," Margaret said. "If the neighbors complain about us screaming and yelling then they're going to hear a gunshot. Duh."

Regina looked around the home. The basement door caught her eye.

"We'll lead him down there," Regina said, leading her sister down the basement steps. "Nobody can hear anything down here. The noise will be drowned out."

"Here," Margaret said, removing some blue tarp from the shelf. She spread the material down on the basement floor in front of the steps. "We can't leave any blood stains."

"Check you out," Regina laughed. "Miss Perry Mason."

Margaret laughed as she flattened out the tarp, placing it in a perfect line with the basement stairs. "Okay," she said, walking halfway up the steps. "So if we shoot him from here," pointing her forefinger into a gun. "He'll fall straight down there."

"Perfect."

The two sisters giggled and gave each other fist bump.

"Here is where the disconnect took place," Clark said. "They had embraced an environment and a culture where there were a lot of faux tough guys. Guys who said they would commit violence but for the most part it was all talk. The girls took it literally. At no point did they realize the gravity of what they were doing. They wanted to be 'gangstas', they wanted to be seen as 'hard'. They didn't have the maturity or the experience to realize that all of those 'gangstas' that they look up to are in jail. They didn't see Oscar at all. He was less than human. Something that is used, discarded and desecrated when it is no longer of use."

CHAPTER FOUR

Oscar was surprised that Regina finally called him back.

"Hey," she said, her teenaged voice soft and inviting.

"You're out of jail?" he asked.

"Yeah," she said. "I really appreciate what you did for me. That was really sweet of you."

"No worries," he said. "I need my money back. Been calling you like crazy."

"I'm sorry, I've just been busy."

"Yeah, I understand. But I need my money back."

"I was wondering if there was some other way I can pay you back?" she said in a sensual tone of voice.

"Like?"

"Like, I know you think my sister is hot, right?"

"What's that got to do with anything?"

"It is something we've been thinking about," she said. "But if you're not cool with it, it's okay."

"Not cool with what?"

"We were wondering if," Regina giggled. "If you can come over for a threesome."

Oscar couldn't believe his luck. He had heard of white girls being freaky, he just didn't think he would ever be able to experience it himself.

Naive to their plan, he rushed over and parked his car outside their mother's home in the South Side of Chicago.

He knocked on the door and was greeted by Margaret and Veronica Garcia, a friend of the two sisters. He didn't see the .38 caliber semi-automatic pistol had in her back waistband.

"Does anyone else know you're coming over?" Margaret asked.

"No," Oscar mumbled, shrugging his shoulder.

Margaret nodded her head and let the young man in. He saw Regina step into the room holding a bin of dirty laundry.

An awkward silence ensued followed by even more awkward smiles. The two sisters fed off each others willingness to go through with the plan. Even if one of them had second thoughts, they would be deemed "soft" by the other.

They had to go through with the murder.

Both women looked over at the young man with come hither looks. Regina said nothing as she opened the basement door and walked down.

"You go with Regina," Margaret said smiling.

"Right," Oscar said, his heart pounding in anticipation as he followed her down.

Oscar heard Margaret's footsteps behind him. What he didn't know was that she had a gun pointed at the back of his head.

When he reached the bottom step, she pulled the trigger.

The young man died instantly, falling face first in the tarp.

"Holy shit!" Margaret said. "I had no idea it would be that fucking loud. It doesn't sound that loud on TV."

Margaret came down the stairs. She kicked Oscar in the head hard, sending more blood spraying across the floor and wall.

"Nobody heard," Regina said as she knelt down and began rifling through Oscar's pockets.

"What the fuck was that?" Veronica said, calling down from the top of the basement steps.

"Did you see that? " Margaret asked. "He fell down like a baby!"

The sisters took out his wallet which had over $600 cash. They took his cell phone then ripped off the sterling silver chain from his neck.

"What the fuck happened?" Veronica said, her voice trembling as she came down a few steps.

"We shot his ass," Margaret said. "He's dead. Look at that shit, he's bleeding through his ears."

"Why did you do it?" Veronica screamed. "Why? Oh my God!"

"Shut the fuck up!" Margaret screamed.

"Don't just stand there," Regina commanded. "Come and help."

Their lifelong friend could only watch as the two sisters took out his car keys and wrapped up his body in a flowery bed sheet.

CHAPTER FIVE

"The girls suffered from what I call the 'Lord of the Flies' syndrome," Clark said. "Here they are hanging out with drug dealers, obtaining guns, killing men in the basement. There is no parental figure in sight! They are left to fend for themselves and the end result is murder and mayhem."

With the dead body in the basement, both sisters peeked out their window, waiting for dark.

Confident that the entire neighborhood was asleep, they opened the door and carried Oscar's body out of the home.

The three girls struggled carrying the dead weight, wrapping his body with a comforter and the flowered bed sheet.

They opened up the trunk and placed the body inside.

"What are you guys doing?" a woman yelled from a window across the street.

The girls looked up startled.

"We're getting rid of some furniture" Regina called out. "No worries."

The girls waved at the neighbor as she moved away from the window.

"Nosy bitch," Regina whispered.

Margaret giggled. Veronica still scared, said nothing.

They got into the vehicle and drove to a vacant lot where they took out Oscar's body again.

"This is hard work," Regina complained. "Shit!"

They plopped the body on the ground, looking at it for a beat before Regina reached back into the trunk. She pulled out a bottle of nail polish remover and poured the liquid over the tarp.

"Are you sure that's gonna work?" Margaret asked.

"It says 'highly flammable'," Regina said, shrugging her shoulders.

Margaret lit a match and set the material on fire.

The flame went up immediately, the girls could feel the warmth on their faces in the cold Chicago night.

"Told you this shit would work!" Regina said.

Then as fast as the flame started, it quickly died down.

"Light another one," Regina said.

Margaret threw down another match, getting the flames going again as Regina doused the tarp with the remaining nail polish remover.

Satisfied, the girls quickly got back into the Camaro and drove off.

**

An anonymous call came into police headquarters reporting the fire in the vacant lot. The caller investigated further, however, and saw Oscar's arm sticking out through the fire. He called 911 again with a sense of urgency, telling them of the body.

CHAPTER SIX

When police on scene identified Oscar Velazquez' partially burned body, their initial knee-jerk reaction was that this was the work of a local street gang, a drug deal gone awry. But when they found the nail polish remover bottle, however, they quickly realized that this was the work of amateurs. A jealous girlfriend maybe.

Meanwhile, the DeFrancisco sisters cruised around town over the following days, trying to pawn off the Camaro.

"This is where the sisters make the guys in 'Dumb and Dumber' look like geniuses," Clark said. "They had only pre-planned the front end of the murder. Like most impulsive killers, they had no idea what to do after. Their greed took over and they decide to sell the Camaro. They have no papers for it, duh, and really can only sell a stolen vehicle to a thug. They find no takers as even the dumbest street gang member isn't going to buy a hot car from two teenaged girls. So they cruise around town and Oscar's brother spots them in the car."

The girls, failing in their sales efforts, would later abandon he vehicle behind a storefront and set it on fire.

**

The day after Oscar's killing, a mutual friend named Jessica Benitez stopped by the house. Jessica went downstairs and watched Margaret mop up a stain of blood near the basement steps.

"The hell is that?" she asked.

Margaret said nothing as she poured bleach over the blood, scrubbing hard.

"Dude bled all over the floor," Regina said. "But only after Margaret kicked him in the head. We called him over, told this idiot we'd have a threesome with him. Then we robbed his ass."

"But the blood stain on the floor-" Jessica asked, watching Margaret clean up.

"We killed a guy," Margaret said without remorse.

"He was going to kill us!" Regina said. "Margaret shot him in the back of the head. We searched his body and found a gun in his waistband. Then we wrapped him up in plastic and put him in his car."

"Holy shit, girl," Jessica.

"We're about to go on the run," Margaret announced.

"Aren't you scared?" Jessica asked, looking back down at the blood stain in the basement.

"I ain't scared of nothing," Margaret said. "You should have seen his head when I shot him. His brain oozed out like cheese."

Margaret made a rolling motion with her hands.

Jessica then accompanied Margaret to the store she purchased a bottle of blonde hair dye for her "disguise."

"We see here how the whole street gang culture has influenced the behavior of these girls," Clark said. "At any point in time, Veronica or Jessica could have went straight to the police. But they get caught up in the drama of the moment. The so-called 'loyalty' to their friend who, quite frankly, would shoot them up in a heartbeat if they knew that they were going to be a snitch."

Going off the tip from Oscar's brother, the police show up to question both Regina and Margaret. The duo denied ever seeing Oscar.

They then go to interview Veronica Garcia.

They found the jittery fifteen year old to be a different story, however. The teen quickly crumbled under the pressure of questioning and told the police the entire story.

Feeling the heat, the DeFrancisco sisters go on the run...

CHAPTER SEVEN

For all of their stupidity in committing the murder, the DeFrancisco sisters deftly avoided capture for almost two years.

They decided to split up. Margaret would go to live with their maternal aunt in Roscoe, Illinois, an hour and a half drive away from where they lived. Roscoe was a small town with less then 10,000 people, a far cry from the drug infested streets of Chicago. Margaret's worst dreams were now realized. She was now a nerd who had to stay inside all day long, living in a boring cul-de-sac with no street gang action. Neighbors would remark that they would never see her and if hey did she would quickly go back inside.

Living underground without detection, it took a broadcast of the television show AMERICA'S MOST WANTED to generate an anonymous tip which led to Margaret's whereabouts. Police staked out her aunt's apartment and entered, finding Margaret in her bedroom with a blank look on her face.

"My feelings were hurt bad because she (my wife) did something behind my back," Margaret's uncle by marriage said later. "I knew (police) were going to find her anyway."

Seven months later, Regina was captured in Dallas living with her Latin King boyfriend, Johnny Rivera.

Initially, she did not even know where the gang banger lived. She just knew the town, Laredo, and she journeyed there by bus. Regina would eventually find him, locating one of his relatives. She would live under an alias and claimed that she worked as a maid.

Police knew better. Regina made money by selling drugs under the Latin King banner.

Unlike Margaret, Regina had evaded the scrutiny of the America's Most Wanted viewers.

Her capture came about because she could not stop hanging out with the wrong crowd.

Two sheriffs were had mistakenly arrived at her boyfriend's apartment, wanting to serve a warrant to someone else.

Rivera allowed the deputies to enter his apartment but he had left a marijuana flake on his table. Police searched the apartment further and found several packages of crack cocaine ready to be sold.

The deputies arrested Rivera. They searched inside the apartment and interviewed Regina, who was groggy from a cocaine high. She showed them her false Texas identification and they let her go.

But the deputies smelled something fishy on her aside from marijuana. They had the apartment manager set up a meeting with her. She arrived at the complex in an SUV with another man. The police approached and the SUV sped away.

The high-speed chase down residential Dallas streets reached upwards of 90 mph. The SUV then slammed into a center median, the front tires blowing out.

Regina got out of the car and tried to sprint away. A deputy tackled her and they fell to the ground, her cell phone skidding across the gravel road. Sifting through her pockets, the officer found over $1,500 cash.

She was taken to Dallas County Jail where they discovered her true identity.

"We pulled her out of jail," said a Deputy Dodson. "I asked to see one of her tattoos, and she showed me...I called her by name, but she never said a word to me. She knew it was over."

She was then extradited to Illinois to stand trial for the murder of Oscar Velazquez.

CHAPTER EIGHT

The trial of the two women began in July of 2004 and both sisters pleaded not guilty by reason of self-defense.

But their friend, Veronica Garcia, had cut a deal with prosecutors in return for a lesser sentence. She would provide the testimony that would damn the two sisters to prison.

Garcia said that she didn't know what the sisters had planned. She had simply provided the gun to the DeFrancisco's which she thought would be used for a robbery only.

"I didn't see her shoot Oscar," Veronica said.

The prosecution brought forth additional witnesses in Jessica Benitez, Luciana Macias, and Maria Constantino, the neighbor.

"Both of them told me that they killed Oscar," Jessica said. "Margaret kicked him in the head so he could die faster."

"I saw them load the body into the back of the Camaro," Constantino said. "Regina told me that she planned out the killing."

Margaret, however, maintained their innocence. She said that Oscar came to the apartment angry because the sisters had tricked him out of one-thousand dollars.

"I shot him to protect Regina," Margaret said.

"Then why didn't you tell the reporting officer what happened?" the prosecution attorney asked.

"We would've got in trouble," Margaret said. "If I told the truth, I would've been there longer."

Regina DeFrancisco would also take the stand and claim self-defense as well.

"I came out of my bedroom," Regina said. "And he was there, cursing and screaming. He pulled a gun on me. I thought I was going to die. I curled up on the floor, in a fetal position. I begged for my life. Then I heard a gunshot and saw Margaret standing over Oscar, holding a gun."

"Whose idea was it to dispose of the body?"

"Veronica knew of this vacant lot," Regina said. "It was her idea."

The jury would deliberate for over six and a half hours. Regina would be found guilty of murder. Margaret's jury, however, was unable to convict her. There was and 11 to 1 deadlock with one juror believing that she should be acquitted. The juror did not believe that someone so young could commit murder.

Margaret was then released from custody and told to await retrial. She had a baby during this time, a girl, and would find work as a nursing assistant while she awaited another trial.

Four months later, Margaret would be given another day in court. Veronica Garcia would once again be the star witness for the prosecution, detailing the exact same testimony as before.

There would be no deadlock in this second go around as Margaret would be convicted of first-degree murder.

Regina would be sentenced to 35 years in prison while Margaret would be sentenced to 46 years. Both women are now jailed at the Dwight Correctional Center. They have each filed appeals which have been denied.

"The girls cared nothing about Oscar Velazquez," Clark said. "In the end, they remained true to their own narcissistic nature. They only cared about what was happening to the next. They cared about nothing about the now fatherless children Oscar Velazquez would leave behind nor about the fact that the took his life."

Veronica Garcia was jailed for five years. She served her full sentence and has since been released.

"This is a cautionary tale if there ever was one," Clark said. "The sisters had it all. They had access to one of the finest schools in their state. Yet they chose to throw it all away for short money and the cheap thrill of the 'thug life.' In the end, they got to see what the 'thug life' was really all about. Mindless violence where everyone is out for themselves, especially when there is a plea bargain to be made. They could have had it all had they stayed on the straight and narrow. Now they have nothing."

WITCH KILLERS : THE TRUE STORY OF SUZAN AND MICHAEL CARSON

TAMMY BENNETT

"What started as two hippies going on an acid trip that quickly evolved into a serial killing couple. Suzan thought that she was giving a vision by Allah. She could go on to kill homosexuals and witches. The two then imagined themselves to be these heroic martyrs battling the forces of evil. They were nothing more than schizophrenic killers."

"Oh God!"

"Sir, what is the address?" the police dispatcher asked for the second time.

"She's dead. There's blood everywhere. Everywhere."

The panicked landlord had just discovered the body of his tenant in her basement apartment in San Francisco. She was lying face down in a pool of blood, covered by a blanket.

Her name was Keryn Barnes. Twenty-three years old with long blonde hair and wholesome features that looked like someone you would meet at a church social.

The landlord had enlisted the aid of a plumber to go investigate the basement apartment he owned on Schrader Street in San Francisco. He had not heard or seen the lovely young woman that he had rented the place out to and was worried about her.

His worst fears would soon become realized.

Police would find no signs of forced entry and Keryn still had money in her purse. She did not appear to have been raped.

Keryn had sustained several blows to the head which caused a skull fracture. The coroner found a bloodied iron skillet in the kitchen cabinet and upon further examination determined that the young woman suffered twelve to thirteen stab wounds to the neck and face.

The apartment wall was painted with mysterious religious symbols, spiral shaped ankhs, triangles and other arcane drawings.

On the bottom of one wall, however, netted one clue.

The name "Suzan" was scrawled in black ink.

Police would go on to interview some of Keryn Barnes' friends and they would find out that the young woman had taken in a strange couple by the name of Michael and Suzan Bear. Keryn had met the two hippies at a party in the Haight-Ashbury district, becoming immediate friends.

"I know something about you," Suzanne said to the young Keryn. "You're anxious. You're curious. I know because I used to be like you. You know, searching. But Michael and I we got something, man. All you have to do is sit still. Sit still and let the power of the universe flow inside you."

Keryn listened in rapt attention as the older woman passed the joint to her.

"That's right," Michael said, eyeballing the blonde beauty in front of him. She was younger than Suzan but he could not bring himself to lust after another woman. Or could he? "This culture we live in, our minds and bodies have become disconnected. There's a whole conspiracy to set minds apart from our true selves. Mind and body have to be one. We have to fight against all of the evil forces that prevent that from happening."

Barnes loved the counterculture of the San Francisco scene and felt a kinship with the weird couple. These were the kind of people she wanted to meet, so different from the people she grew up in Georgia. They had their own belief systems and were not constrained by polite society.

In her eyes, they were "cool."

The Bears would talk to Keryn about transcendental meditation, psychic phenomena and their own interpretation of the Muslim religion in which the young woman found fascinating. The two hippies needed a place "to crash for a little while" and Keryn took pity on the duo, allowing them to stay with her.

She slowly became drawn into their way of thinking, becoming their acolyte but having no idea how dangerous they really were.

The Bears had no criminal record but they were about to embark on a murder spree in which they would avoid capture for over two years.

And Keryn Barnes would be their first victim.

SUZAN CARSON

On the surface, Suzanne Carson lived an otherwise normal life growing up in Arizona in the 1950s. Her father was a newspaper executive while her mother was a housewife. As she grew older, however, she became more reclusive. She truly believed she was psychic and because of her introverted nature she had very few friends. Suzanne did very poorly in school, suffering from severe dyslexia.

Suzanne would marry, becoming a housewife just like her own mother. She lived in Scottsdale but she did not put on the false front of being happily married. She had a teenage son and often flirted with his friends.

She had the life of privilege, her husband was wealthy and she would spend her afternoons playing tennis. In the end, however, Suzanne was accustomed to the wealth from both her upbringing and now her marriage. She wanted something more. She wanted power, authority and attention.

A sexual predator, she played the role of "Mrs.Robinson" to her son's high school classmates, shamelessly flirting and going out on "dates" with them. In later interviews, she would brag that she bedded "over one-hundred fifty" of her son's classmates. These sexual rendezvous were intensified with her use of hallucinogenic drugs (acid, peyote, hash, marijuana).

Suzanne went on an acid trip with one of her son's high school friends then woke up in the morning to find her entire living room painted in red triangles with the name "Suzan" written at the bottom. Not remembering what she did the previous evening, Suzanne claimed that there was "a hole in my head" and that "all of the electricity in the house" was now flowing through her.

Suffering from these delusions, Suzanne would describe her own visual hallucinations.

"Suzanne was a schizophrenic," forensic psychologist Paula Flowers said. "It grew worse as she got older and she obviously needed psychiatric assistance. She needed to have been diagnosed, medicated and perhaps even institutionalized. But this was the early 1980s and we didn't have a lot of the mental health precautions in place like we have now. She was, in essence, a functional schizophrenic. The people she came in contact with would write off her strange ramblings as coming from someone who was a 'bit off'. And when she moved to San Francisco she fit right in."

"We can argue that Suzanne may have been medicating herself with the daily use of drugs," Flowers said. "Her use of hallucinogenic drugs increased as the years went on. She would have 'visions' as she would call them but a doctor would call them delusions and consider her to be very, very dangerous. When you combine acid tripping with schizophrenia you can get a lethal cocktail and that is what we got with Suzan. The drugs would only enhance her bizarre visions and make things much worse."

Suzan grew tired of the role as a housewife while her husband grew tired of her bizarre thought processes and behavior. Her husband would divorce her and take his two children with him. She was now free to embrace the counterculture and free love philosophy that she always wanted.

She began developing her own radical interpretation of the Islamic religion and with her new found identity she changed her name from

Suzanne to Suzan, thinking that the mess she created in the living room was some kind of sign from Allah.

Suzan took bits and pieces from the Islamic religion to fit her own needs as she enjoyed mescaline and marijuana. Square jawed and wild eyed, Suzan began losing her physical attractiveness and noticed that the teenage boys no longer paid too much attention to her.

She needed a new man.

Around the age of 35, she went through a serious acid trip and began to have visions. These visions called for her to have a spiritual partner to "complete her destiny".

She would meet this man in James Carson.

JAMES CARSON

James Carson was born in 1950 in Oklahoma. He grew up in a normal middle class family. His father was an oil engineer while his mother was a schoolteacher.

His childhood was typical until he was diagnosed with a rare bone disorder when he was very young. He was put on bed rest for several years where he devoured books of philosophy, religion, politics and history.

He grew to have a combative personality, however, regularly using drugs and alcohol.

"Part of James' mental illness was that he thought everyone was about to get him," Flowers said. "There would be no way in hell he could hold down a job. He was anti-social and argumentative, willing to take offense at the most minor details."

James would take a stab at normalcy, however, as he would meet a woman named Lynn at the University of Iowa where he obtained a masters degree in Chinese studies. The couple married, had a child, then moved to Arizona.

His wife worked while James stayed at home to take care of his young daughter. He was a loving father but his anti-social tendencies ran deep. He hated the government, believed in conspiracies and soon became impossible to live with. Lynn divorced James and soon afterward he met Suzan.

Long-haired and bearded, James cut a Charles Manson-esque appearance. His eyes were empty and soulless, often greeting people with an expressionless glare.

CRAZY AND CRAZIER

When the two first met at a party, there was instant chemistry. Suzan was nine years older, taking on the mother/God role that James seemed to be looking for. He loved Buddhist philosophy and had been waiting his whole life for a woman like Suzan, someone who turned her back on mainstream American values. Suzan liked younger men, she liked being looked upon as a mother figure, a spiritual guide that led young men into drug-crazed nights where she was the center of their world.

Suzan was looking for someone to worship her and she found that in James who made her feel sexually attractive again.

"They both described their meeting as instant electric attraction," Jenn Carson said, the daughter of James. "From that very moment that they met, they were just joined like magnets."

"Me and you," Suzan said meeting James for the first time. "We're the same."

"That right?"

"There is a defiance in you. You are who you are and you are going to stick to your guns. We're the same, you and I. There is a whole world out there that is trying to suffocate who we are. We can fight back. We can take our swords into battle together."

Suzan saw James as a reflection of who she was and the two begin a daily routine of pot, alcohol and hallucinogenic drugs. They would have daily discussions on the problems of the world and how only they understood it.

James, in essence, becomes Suzan's follower in their cult of two. They both had the same spiritual fantasies and they both suffered from mental illness.

Baptizing James into her self-made religion, Suzan decided that he should change his name. She christened him as "Michael", in reference to the archangel from the Bible who fought demons. They adopt the last name of "Bear" as James may have used his childhood fascination with the animals as inspiration.

"What we see happening is a reinvention of themselves," Flowers said. "By taking on these new identities they shed all of the ghosts of their past. Renaming themselves was a symbolic gesture, their way of taking control and being rid of the societal forces that they felt were keeping them down. They were free to recreate a new person and that person would have power. That person would be special, given a license from God himself to go and rid the world of evil."

The couple would go on acid trips and engage in their own invented prayer sessions. They would talk in tongues, read from selected verses in the Koran and then indulge in yoga-inspired chants. Michael was well-versed in eastern religions but again followed Suzan's lead as she went from one discipline to another in her mescaline-fueled prayer sessions.

"My father had always been interested in very radical religious beliefs," Jenn Carson said. "Those interests became more and more extreme."

"It was the most bizarre environment you can imagine. It was like being dropped into a rabbit hole. You have two individuals who both have mental health needs and now they're using very, very heavy drugs."

Suzanne would have visions, seeing kaleidoscopic lights through trees, strange elephant like creatures and ancient bronze statues with no form.

"Suzan truly believed that she was going crazy," Flowers said. "She had to recognize that her own brain was not functioning properly so perhaps that is why she believed that there was a divine entity that was telling her to commit these acts. She thought everyone was out to get them. The FBI was out to get them. A secret government agency was out to get them. Yet Allah is the force that is on their side."

Michael convinced her, however, that her delusions were a gift. Like an old time Biblical prophet, Suzanne was chosen to receive these visions from Allah.

"You're a prophet," Michael said with excitement. "You're a yogi. You're not a witch. You have been given privileged access. Your visions are a gift!"

"Maybe you're right," Suzan rubbed her head.

"There's a reason why Allah is invisible. Have you ever thought about that? No one else can see him. But you can hear him."

"There's a war coming," Suzan said. "God will send someone to fight the Evil. And that someone is us. That's what he's saying to me."

"That's right."

"Everyone will die," Suzan said, lowering her voice just in case someone from the government was listening. "Everyone who practices witchcraft. Homosexuals. Witches. All of the evil people. We have to look beyond ourselves. The police. The government. Celebrities and politicians. Every bad person will burn in fire!"

The vision fit in line with Michael's own paranoid schizophrenic personality. He saw witches everywhere, the government, the media, the person on the street.

Deluded and convinced of their own righteousness, they became a "cult" of two.

The duo would move to California for a new life, settling into the Haight-Ashbury district.

"They were on the hunt for new recruits," Flowers said. "I don't think they had clarity as to the type of person they were going for, male or female. They were simply looking for someone young and open-minded."

They would meet Keryn Barnes at the party and she would take the couple in.

"She (Keryn) was kind of interested in that eclectic scene," Jenn Carson said. "And she was very much a bohemian girl. When Suzan and Michael entered her life I think she found them fascinating."

"Keryn was young and impressionable," Flowers said. "She had embraced that whole San Francisco counterculture mentality where you do not judge anyone. She probably didn't see herself as a follower in their cult. She wanted some older people to hang out with, people who were different from her. She could not see what anyone in their right mind could see in Suzan and Michael. They were weird, crazy and dangerous."

Suzan, however, would grow jealous of the beauty of Keryn. She would notice the sideways glances that Michael would give the pretty and young Keryn.

"Suzan would look in the mirror and see an old lady with yellow teeth," Flowers said. "She wore no make-up and she had thick jawline with deepening wrinkles. She compared herself to the young Keryn and felt inferior."

Fearing that she would lose Michael, she began brainwashing her younger lover into believing that Keryn was a witch.

"Do you think she's pretty?" Suzan asked as Michael watch Keryn head into the bathroom.

"Yeah," he said, nodding his head without commitment.

"Keryn's a witch," Suzan said.

"No," Michael said. "Keryn is cool, man."

"She's siphoning away my youth," Suzan said. "Taking away my powers as a yogi. She's trying to come between us. I can feel it. She's doing it psychically. I know she is."

"What?"

"She's a witch. She must be dealt with."

"No."

"We have to kill the witch," Suzan said, looking deep her lover's eyes. "Michael, you have to kill Keryn."

"Suzan truly believed she had psychic powers," Flowers said. "She would look Michael directly in his eyes and try and communicate to him through telepathy. She thought she had ESP. He would always comply so his obedience would only provide further evidence that she did have psychic powers."

Repressing his growing lust for Keryn like any good religious disciple, Michael would obey his mother figure in Suzan.

On March 7th, 1981, Michael Bear Carson would kill Keryn Barnes, attacking her with a frying skillet as she slept on the floor.

He fractured her skill before stabbing her with a paring knife.

"Suzan and Michael portrayed Keryn as a witch," Jenn Carson said. "As a woman who was trying to break up a marriage. None of those things were true. This was a nice girl from Georgia. No one should go through what she went through. She was beautiful, delightful twenty-three year old girl."

"All of the crazy and deluded talk they have done has now come to a head," Flowers said. "They've just killed their first 'witch'. They both have delusions of grandeur in ridding the world of more 'witches', so away they go to kill as many 'witches' as they can."

Suzan and Michael then went on the run, heading toward Oregon.

They would find an isolated cabin in the woods and enjoy what they would call their own "private paradise". The anti-social couple were away from people and frolicked in the wilderness.

"This was meant to be," Suzan said, twirling around underneath the tall Oregon trees. "This is our reward for being good servants to Allah."

"This is true wealth," Michael said looking across the Oregon landscape, smelling the scent of the jasmine flowers. "Not something that you buy. It is contentment of the soul."

"We can stay here forever," she said. "But let us not forget that we are 'hash-ashins'. Islamic assassins. We must go out and search for more prey. There is still plenty of evil in the world. But this will be our refuge. Our safe-house."

Their delusions were short-lived, however, as the couple soon ran out of food and supplies in the cabin. Michael would hitch-hike into the nearest town where he met a local construction worker who let the couple stay in his tree house.

The man soon felt uncomfortable with the arrangement as Suzan said very little. She would laugh and smile at inappropriate moments. Suzan had a way of looking at a person, she would stare and then smile as if she knew something that the person didn't.

She gave him the creeps.

Sensing that the couple was dangerous, the man sent a thug armed with a gun to kick the couple out as they headed back to California.

They would find a marijuana plantation in California and land a job of care taking the illegal operation in a remote part of Humboldt County.

The couple did not make friends with anyone at the plantation and soon locked horns with a man named Clark Stevens who was part owner. Stevens could be gruff, not averse to four letter words and looked down on hired help hippies like Michael and Suzan.

Michael had an assigned post working security, standing guard at the fence in front of the hidden plantation. Stevens pulled up, honked his horn and demanded to be let into the farm.

"No one is supposed to be here today," Michael said, blocking the front gate as Stevens came out of his jeep.

"That right?" Stevens said. "Who the hell are you?"

"Who the hell are you?" Michael challenged back.

"I own this fucking place!" Stevens said. "Open the fucking gate."

"No," Suzan said. "Michael, you know you can't let him through. It is your job."

"Tell your bitch to shut up and open the fucking gate!" Stevens grew more agitated.

Suzan would see Stevens as a man that needed to be eliminated. Stevens would later criticize the way the hippie couple handled the plants and wanted them out off the plantation. The couple, however, decided to nip the flower in the bud and take care of Stevens themselves.

"He disrespected me," she said to Michael.

"What do you want me to do?"

"He touched me!" Suzan said, the words hissing from her mouth. "Are you going to let him get away with that?"

Suzan detailed a story in which she believed that Stevens had made a sexual pass at her. This gave Michael carte blanche to commit his murder.

Michael then confronted Stevens inside the plantation grounds and shot him in the head.

"Michael shot Stevens on the orders of Suzan," Flowers said. "She thought that Stevens had disrespected her and used Michael as her weapon of choice. That was part of her mental make-up, to use Michael as her hit man, so to speak. If she saw that someone needed eliminating she would snap her fingers and Michael would do her bidding. Disrespecting Suzan would be met with a death sentence."

The two then chopped up Stevens body, doused his body with kerosene and set him on fire.

"Just looking at the level of brutality," Flowers said. "The Stevens murder was a step beyond the Barnes murder with the added desecration of a dismemberment and burning of the corpse. The 'Witch Killers' weren't the type of serial murderers that had a set modus operandi. They were opportunistic and random which is what made them so hard to catch."

Police would later discover Stevens' body by accident when a helicopter spotted one of the dogs playing with what at first glance seemed like a ball.

Looking closer, they realized that the dog was playing with a human head.

The investigating police would later smell the body of Stevens before they saw it. His body had been only partially burned as the couple had covered him up with chicken manure which had been used to fertilize the marijuana plants.

KILLING RONALD REAGAN

The couple began making out a hit list of prominent figures they wanted to kill. At the top of the list stood Ronald Reagan and Johnny Carson.

The couple believed that the first, middle and last names had six letters. They saw supernatural significance in the numbers 666, the designation of the beast.

Still on the run, the couple would drive toward a roadblock. Police had blockaded the road looking for another criminal but the couple had mistakenly believed that the investigation was for them.

They stopped their stolen vehicle and immediately ran into the northern California woods. Deputies gave chase and would see Michael drop his backpack.

Inside his belongings, they would find his book which he titled "Cry For War."

"The book contained passages of Michael's philosophical beliefs," Flowers said. "Rambling on and on, it did attract interest of both the FBI and Secret Service, however, because the book wrote of assassinating the President. So now the deluded couple who imagined that big, black government helicopters were out to get them had to now face the real thing."

CAUGHT BY ACCIDENT

Michael would later be detained by police as he fit the description of a rapist. He had stolen some identification from someone else and gave the police that false information.

The police took his picture and faxed it over to the hospital so the rape victim could make a positive identification.

The victim said hat it wasn't him and Michael was released.

Taking to the road again, the couple began hitch-hiking. They were soon picked up by a man named John Hillyer.

"The couple now had more than a little blood lust in them," Flowers said. "They no longer limited themselves to killing people that they perceived as 'witches'. Now anyone that showed them the slightest amount of disrespect would be in mortal danger."

"You folks need a lift?" Hillyer called out.

Michael gave a thumbs up to the driver, moving toward the vehicle until Suzan stopped him. "He might be a witch," she said. "We're going to have to kill him."

The couple climbed into Hillyer's pick up truck. Suzan sat in between the two men. Hillyer played country music on the radio which Suzan hated.

"Witch music," she whispered.

Then Hillyer's leg accidentally brushed against hers.

Suzan interpreted the touch as a sexual pass. She looked at Michael, gazing deep into his eyes. Without saying a word, she tried to communicate to him through telepathy that he had to kill Hillyer.

Michael said nothing as he took out his gun.

"Hey man," Hillyer said. "What the hell is that?"

Michael hesitated. Then he pointed the gun at Hillyer.

Hillyer grabbed the gun and a struggle ensued. Suzan got into the middle of the fracas, scratching and clawing at the driver.

"The fuck is wrong with you people!" Hillyer screamed.

The fight for the gun continued for ten minutes, Hillyer trying to wrest the weapon away from Michael while Suzan screamed and bit him.

The car skidded to a stop on the highway.

Hillyer stepped out of vehicle, letting go of the gun.

There were witnesses. Surely, this crazed couple would not shoot him in broad daylight with all these people around who could identify them.

Hillyer attempted to sprint over to the side of the road.

"John jumped out to run for his life," Jenn Carson said. "And Suzan and Michael proceeded to both stab and shoot him on the side of the road in full view of commuters driving by. John died on the side of the road."

"John died because Suzan ordered it," Flowers said. "Michael was the willing patsy, a violent enabler, if you will. He did all these things to make her happy. Hillyer had innocently brushed his leg up against Suzan's. In Suzan's demented world, that was a capital offense."

The numerous witnesses, however, allowed the police to positively identify and capture the killers, ending their rampage.

MEDIA COVERAGE

In a bizarre twist, the couple held their own public news conference where they were allowed to detail their deluded philosophy. The two then went on a five-hour televised rant in which they justified their killings as a war on witchcraft.

"We rid the world of evil!" Suzan proclaimed. "Witches. People with dark forces."

"They did talk about the murders," Jenn Carson said. "And laid down this case that they were being spiritually attacked and that they had to defend themselves. That they were called to kill witches, their whole rationale."

The press conference was broadcast by KGO-TV in the San Francisco Bay Area.

"Their delusions were made public," Flowers said. "In hindsight, this really set a wrong precedent as it gave two deluded people a public stage. A part of me thinks that a defense attorney staged this in order to make the case that these two should not be able to competent to stand trial. If that was the case, it didn't work thankfully."

"In looking back, we see these two mentally ill people who were totally convinced in their psychotic beliefs. In their delusions of grandeur, they wanted the world to know of their work."

On June 4th, 1984, Suzan and Michael Carson were found guilty of the first degree murder of Keryn Barnes. Later, they were found guilty of the murders of Clark Stevens and John Hillyer.

Both were sentenced to a total of 75 years to life.

"Michael and Suzan were like dynamite and a match," Jenn Carson said. "Without the other, would this have occurred? I don't know."

Jenn Carson has now come to terms with her father being a serial killer.

"I would describe my father as brilliant," Jenn Carson recalled. "Handsome. Charming. Damaged. Misguided and soulless."

"I think Suzan is intelligent," Jenn Carson said. "And crazy. And evil."

"You absolutely cannot have rehabilitation when there is absolutely no remorse," Carson said. "Neither of these people feel any remorse whatsoever. They speak about it, in a way that almost glamorizes it, and Suzan has bragged about being friends with the Manson girls in prison. There doesn't seem to be any sign whatsoever that they would come out changed in any way."

James Carson is incarcerated at Mule Creek State Prison while Suzan is jailed at the Central California Women's Facility.

They were both up for parole in 2015, becoming eligible because of their age and prison overcrowding.

Both were denied.

9 798224 319008